the
crazy
twins

Surviving Bipolar & Alzheimer's

Spencer Swalm

ILLUMIFY
MEDIA.COM

Published by
Illumify Media Global
www.IllumifyMedia.com
"Let's bring your book to life!"

Paperback ISBN: 978-1-959099-33-8

Typeset by Jennifer Clark
Cover design by Debbie Lewis

Printed in the United States of America

To my loving wife who has endured my Crazy Twins for all these years

CONTENTS

INTRODUCTION

Why did the crazy twins start a band?

Because they were convinced they had perfect harmony, even if nobody else could tell!

And let me tell you, I've lived with crazy twins most of my life.

Their names? Bipolar disorder and dementia. They're convinced they live in perfect harmony, even if nobody else can tell!

These two challenges have tested me in ways that I never thought possible, but I have managed to build a full and meaningful life in spite of them. How did I do it? The answer is simple: the Lord has been merciful to me.

My name is Spencer Swalm, and I am 72 years old. I was born and raised in Denver, and I have been married for 44 years. Together, my wife and I have raised three children and now enjoy the company of six grandchildren. But my life has not always been easy. Living with bipolar disorder and dementia has been a constant struggle, and at times, it has threatened to derail everything I have worked so hard to achieve.

Perhaps you're familiar with one of the twins or some other mental illness. I have good news for you.

Your life is not over. In fact, you can still live a full life, bursting with adventure and meaning.

Despite my many challenges, I have managed to persevere. I have served in the Colorado House of Representatives, built a successful career as an entrepreneur, and maintained strong relationships with my family and friends.

In this book, I share my story - the ups, the downs, and everything in between - in the hopes that it will inspire and encourage others who are living with mental illness.

Through personal stories, reflections, and practical advice, I offer a glimpse into the ways in which I have found meaning, purpose, and joy in the midst of chaos. I share the strategies that have helped me to manage my symptoms and live a fulfilling life, and offer a message of hope to those who are struggling to find their way.

Please join me in this journey.

Living with bipolar disorder and dementia—or any mental illness—is not easy, but it is possible to build a life that is rich, rewarding, and full of love. With God's mercy and grace, anything is possible.

WRITE WHAT YOU KNOW AND
WHAT OTHERS WANT TO LEARN

Over a tasty plate of pad thai at Tuk Tuk, I had a heart to heart with Kathie Reiner, the lady who's been helping me with this blog for years.

"Spencer," she said in her very matter-of-fact way, "if you ever want your blog to be anything more than a hobby, you have to very specifically identify what interests your readers, and then help them solve their problems. We've talked about this before. You know how to write. But you have to get and stay focused. You can't jump from topic to topic if you ever want to get anywhere. In the world of social media, it's called addressing an avatar."

"Yes," I replied, "and I know I've pretty much ignored your advice. But I've been giving it some thought. And I'm ready to clean up my act.

"You know I'm bipolar. And have been for decades. I've blogged about it. When I was in my early twenties, I was involuntarily committed to a psychiatric hospital for two or three weeks."

"And I'm not alone. Millions of Americans suffer from some form of mental illness. And when you add in the family members and loved ones that have to deal with the consequences of those disorders, there are countless more impacted by mental health issues. I could write posts on this topic," I concluded, "until the cows come home. And come nowhere near exhausting the subject."

I've eaten quite a lot of Asian food over the last few years. My daughter's married to great guy who's half Korean, and I don't think they ever turn off their rice cooker. So, I've become quite adept at chop sticks; I was done with my pad thai before Kathie was done with whatever she was eating with her fork.

"But, you know," I said between mouthfuls, "does this mean that I have to quit posting about political issues altogether?"

"No," she answered, "politicians deal with mental health issues all the time. You probably voted on some yourself."

"Very true," I answered, laying aside my chop sticks for a moment. "They came up routinely."

"But to start with," continued Kathie, "you need to make it clear to your readers, your avatars, that you're headed in a new direction. And when you do post on politics, start by focusing on those issues that intersect with mental health. After that, when you've built up a following of tens of thousands," she said with a sly smile, "go anywhere your heart desires. Just not too often."

So, there you have it. My blog, more or less, had a focus on mental health issues. And this book is a collection of the blog posts that focus more, not less, on my brain struggles: one of which I've had basically all my life, bipolar. The other being a recent dilemma, incipient dementia—or Alzheimer's. I hope you will be encouraged by my stories with these crazy twins.

WHY "FORMERLY HONORABLE"?

I was at the dentist's getting my teeth cleaned today. As is the customary practice in such circumstances, the pleasant young hygienist asked me a question that I couldn't answer till I had finished swishing out my mouth and she had sucked the fluid away with the little straw.

"Are you still in the legislature?"

"No," I replied, flat on my back, peering through the protective dark glasses, "I was term limited out of office last January." Before she plunged her hands back in my mouth, I managed to get out, "You can now call me the 'formerly honorable'."

She chuckled. "So you haven't done anything wrong? But what did you think of your time down at the capital? Was there anything in particular you were able to accomplish?"

My answer, while necessarily abbreviated, was the one I usually give: it was a great eight-year run. I wouldn't have missed it. But I was also ready to move on; I've gone back to my insurance business, and we have a wonderful new grand-daughter (our first), who lives just down the road. Did I achieve anything of note? I bobbed and weaved: I was only one of a hundred Colorado legislators. But I met a bunch of wonderful people; it's almost impossible not to when you have spent countless hours during four campaigns knocking on countless doors talking to countless constituents.

So the plan is that this blog will play some part in the next stage of this formerly honorable politician's life. Give me a platform to comment, occasionally, on those things that I think need commenting on. Maybe even on the hygienist herself, a bright, lovely young woman three years married who, when I ventured that her parents would probably like to see grand-kids of their own replied, "We like our life as it is. And we like our dogs."

Go figure. And stay tuned.

3

BROTHER, CAN YOU SPARE A DIME?

This last Sunday evening I made a quick trip to our local, suburban grocery store. As I left the nearly empty parking lot and waited at the red light to turn on to Arapahoe Road, a young/old woman stood to my left holding a worn cardboard sign that read, "Single mom need help."

I quickly went through the usual mental gymnastics: Are you really a single mom? If I give you a dollar, will it just go up in smoke or something worse? Or really help the kids? That she was a woman cinched it for me; I don't give money to men standing at stop lights.

I pushed the down button on the passenger window and said, "Hey, I have something for you." I hurriedly pulled a dollar from my wallet; the light could change any time. She acted like she hadn't heard me; she could hardly see my car, let alone me, with the sun just above the mountains to the west blasting into her eyes. I tried again, louder, "Ma'am, here's a dollar."

She heard me this time and took off the dark glasses that were doing a poor job of protecting her from the glare. "Sorry," she said, coming closer. "I couldn't see you."

She reached into the car; I handed her the bill. She thanked me and backed away. The light changed. And I pulled onto Arapahoe.

What is our city, and country, coming to?

I grew up in Denver. The only memory I have as a youth of panhandlers is one I would like to forget. In high school, some friends and I went down to skid row, which, believe it or not, was where Larimer Square is now. We brought some pliers, some dimes, and some matches. We had a "great" time watching the wretches on the sidewalk burn themselves as they scrambled to pick up the coins we pitched out the windows.

Aside from that shameful experience, I have no recollection of begging in this town back then. But now it is commonplace to see one, two, or even three ragged souls at intersections holding up limp cardboard signs throughout the city. Even in quite suburban areas on a quiet Sunday evening.

Do I know what to do about it? No.

But I do have some thoughts on causes.

First, broken families spawn broken people. In a whole range of ways, virtually every study agrees that divorce or bearing children out of wedlock negatively impacts everyone involved. Divorced parents and single mothers are more likely to be in poverty. Which, of course, spills down to the children. But the problems kids face go beyond poverty. Children in these scenarios are more likely to do poorly in school, be involved in crime, act out sexually, and abuse drugs.

Will a stable marriage solve all these problems? And mean that we see fewer panhandlers on Denver streets? Almost certainly not. But how could it hurt to set it as a goal?

Second, undiagnosed mental illness often plays a role in panhandling and homelessness. And this is something I am qualified to speak about from personal experience. I am bipolar. In my early twenties I was involuntarily committed to a psychiatric hospital for two weeks and put on medication. But like many in my situation, when I was released, I quit taking the medication. "I don't need that stuff."

For the next thirty years I was on a roller coaster. Sometimes maniacally high. But much more frequently in the grip of the black dog of depression. True, I was never homeless, but I was suicidal many times. But I was blessed to be surrounded by a supportive family that was more than enough reason to keep living. Now I see a psychiatrist quarterly and take daily medication. But take it from me, mental illness is debilitating.

I can see how someone can wind up on a street corner holding up a "Single mom need help" sign. But what to do about it is another matter.

4

ON PINS AND NEEDLES

One of the many bills I heard when serving on the Health, Insurance, and Environment Committee when I represented Centennial in the Colorado House dealt with ear acupuncture. The testimony, which I initially took with a grain of salt—actually, a truck load of salt—was that sticking pins in the ears of someone suffering from mental illness could effect a cure, or at least relieve the symptoms.

I began to sit up and take notice when the witnesses, including a woman named MK Christian, began talking about the work they were doing at the state mental hospital in Pueblo. She made it sound as if they were having considerable success. And, when more conventional, allopathic doctors supported their claims, it really got my attention. They said it helped the patients sleep better and reduced their dependence on medication.

I am bipolar. As is fairly typical, I originally manifested the illness as a young adult. While Churchill's black dog of depression was my more usual companion, I had bouts of mania as well. External events often contribute to and exacerbate the mood swings, which was certainly the case with me.

In my early twenties I broke up with a long-time girlfriend.

I was desperate, suicidal, broken on the rock of my sin. I wondered into a church and less than an hour later came out as a newly minted Christian. It was as if someone had popped the top of a champaign bottle; I was effervescent.

Unfortunately, a few days later I went on a pheasant hunting trip with my father and some of his friends. Believe it or not, guns and mania don't work all that well together. No one got hurt, but my father, understandably, was deeply concerned about some of my bizarre behavior.

On our return to Denver, my folks had me involuntarily committed. I was driven to the Mount Airy Psychiatric hospital in the back of a Denver sheriff's squad car. It was, no doubt, the right thing to do. But I felt like a blood brother to McMurphy in *One Flew Over the Cuckoo's Nest*. They put me on medication. I was compliant in the group sessions and met with the psychiatrist, Dr. Walker, whose testimony had convinced the probate court to commit me. When I got out two weeks later, I'd had enough of the drugs and didn't believe I need more counseling. In fact, I really thought that it was my parents that should be seeing a shrink. So like many in my situation, I quit taking the medication. And seeing Dr. Walker.

It was a very long and winding road from there to the point when, in my fifties, I finally was willing to admit I needed help. It began with another bout of mania that reduced my two wonderful daughters to tears, which predictably was followed by a visit from the snarling black dog. But it was still a struggle for my long-suffering wife to persuade me to try to find a psychiatrist.

Fortunately for me, and unfortunately for my former partner, he had a son with similar but even more severe problems. He referred me to a Dr. Jay Carlson. He was smart, with a gentle and yet probing sense of humor. It didn't take Dr. Carlson long to get me on a course of medication that worked —most of the time—and which didn't have too many side effects.

By the time I heard the bill on auricular acupuncture, I certainly knew enough about the illness to be aware that adequate sleep was an important component to keeping the beast at bay. When the testimony was over, I found MK in the crowded hallway outside the committee room and asked for her card.

Within a few days I was in her quaint, old Victorian on Franklin Street, lying face down on a table, staring at the floor through a head rest while she kept up a reassuring patter as she put needles in my scalp, ears, neck, back, and ankles. "There," she said with what I soon learned was characteristic enthusiasm, "that will be a good treatment for you, guy! Now, you rest!" With that, she dimmed the lights, put a heat lamp on my feet, and turned on some soothing music on the Bose.

I woke up about an hour later. I don't think I was drooling —or snoring—that time. But I know on subsequent treatments I have done both.

How does it work? I have no idea. I'm not really convinced that MK does either.

When my daughter couldn't get pregnant she was referred to an acupuncturist by one of the high-tech, high-cost infertility clinics she and her husband had begun seeing. They got pregnant with acupuncture instead. And now they have a second little daughter—this time without any intervention.

One time, I asked MK, "How does acupuncture help with infertility?" Her answer? "I'm not really sure."

Has acupuncture cured my bipolar? No. I still take daily medication. And, especially in the dark days of winter, the black dog can still nip at my heels. But I do think it helps me sleep better.

By the way, on a wall in her clinic is a picture of MK looking over the shoulder of Governor Hickenlooper as he signed the auricular acupuncture bill into law.

5

WET, WACKY, AND WOBBLY

I first noticed it while going door to door in my fourth and last campaign for House District 37 in 2012. Because the district was very competitive, every two years I had to ring thousands of Republican and unaffiliated doorbells between April and Election Day in early November.

Under the best of circumstances, campaigning in this fashion is always time intensive. If I got to one hundred houses in eight hours on a Saturday, I was doing well. It would be fewer houses on weekdays after work, even if I stayed out 'til is was nearly dark on the long summer days.

But after having done so much of it, it wasn't hard for me to sense that it was taking longer to go from house to house than it had during previous campaigns. True, it was never a short walk between houses because cutting across lawns was, according to my mentor and master campaigner, David Balmer, strictly verboten: "It's ok for the mailman. But you don't want to let your constituents see a politician walking across their manicured, suburban grass."

So, I would take the sidewalk to the driveway, up the drive to where the walk forked off to the front porch, up (usually) a few stairs, and ring the bell. Then wait to see if someone answered. If they did, especially on Saturdays, they might want to talk for several minutes. And then reverse the process to the next house. Again, under ideal circumstances, it was slow going.

But try as I might, I couldn't walk as fast as I had in prior campaigns. It felt like there was stickum on the bottom of my shoes. And, just as weird, was the fact that I wasn't comfortable walking down even a few stairs unless there was a handrail.

"What was going on? I was an expert alpine skier, wasn't I? I could ride my mountain bike on rugged single-track trails. I'd backpacked all over the state on rocky, rutted trails. Heck, in my youth I had been a technical rock climber. And now a few stairs were making me nervous?"

It hit me again with equal force when the session got underway the following winter. Legislators interact with lobbyists routinely; I was no different. Many of them are very professional-looking women who work the marble hallways of the capital all day (and sometimes late into the night) in stiletto heels; it looks brutally uncomfortable. But I couldn't keep pace with these women as we walked the seventy-five paces from the house chamber to my office.

I couldn't walk as fast as a woman several inches shorter than me, in high heels. What's going on? Frustration is scarcely adequate to describe my feelings.

I began talking to my doctors.

Maybe the titanium hip that had been put in several years before was going bad. The orthopedic surgeon who did the implant X-rayed it and tested my blood for some sort of titanium poisoning.

Nothing.

The same result when I talked to my GP at an annual physical.

I see a psychiatrist about once a quarter for my bipolar condition. I complained to him. "Can my medication be making me walk like this and not feel secure going down stairs?"

He did a simple battery of physical tests, like balancing on one foot and walking a straight line down the hallway in his office while he watched. Nothing. (After we later learned what was really going on, he repeatedly offered a mea culpa for his oversight. He's a brain doctor after all.)

After complaining a few more times in subsequent visits, he finally decided I needed to see a neurologist and gave me a referral. It took a while to get in, but the appointed day finally arrived; my wife and I sat in the waiting room.

It didn't strike me as odd until later, but the doctor didn't have his nurse escort us to an exam room for the usual preliminaries. Instead, he personally met us in the waiting room and watched me get out of my chair and walk across the room.

I'm convinced he knew what I had even before I got across the room. Of course, some tests had to be run—brain imaging followed by a spinal tap—to confirm his impression. (Take it from me, you haven't lived until you have had an evening to think about a spinal tap before it's done the following morning.)

But sure enough, the initial diagnosis was right: normal pressure hydrocephalus (NPH). Sometimes referred to as the wet, wacky and wobbly syndrome because of the most common symptoms. I'll simply say that I had the first and the third. And add that I hope to be able to avoid the second.

The usual treatment was what was prescribed for me: another hole in my head to implant a shunt to drain excess fluid from my skull to my abdominal cavity where it is reabsorbed.

Has the shunt been a miracle cure? Not hardly. In fact, I have sometimes been resentful when I read stories of others in my situation that do seem to experience full recoveries. But there is no doubt that the shunt has slowed the progression of the condition.

Thankfully, the wet has definitely improved.

Am I wacky? I suppose some might say so. But I contend that I'm still cogent. At least I hope so. And hope to continue to be for a good while beyond what is my sixty-sixth year.

Unfortunately, I'm still wobbly, especially going down stairs; I religiously cling to the hand rail when one is available. But I work out regularly and vigorously, including twice a week with a trainer. He hounds me mercilessly on my posture, virtual posture Nazi. And how could this possibly do anything but help?

NPH has made me more observant of the old people around me (I grow old... I grow old... I shall wear the bottoms of my trousers rolled.). The stooped posture. The shuffling, wide gait. The caution at the curb.

It took the doctors years to figure out what was wrong with me. And I am certainly not alone. The Hydrocephalus Association estimates that of the seven hundred thousand American with NPH, fewer than 20% receive an appropriate diagnosis. NPH is commonly misdiagnosed as Alzheimer's or Parkinson's disease. Or simple aging. But the facts are that it is one of the few causes of dementia that can be treated.

The penultimate take away? If you, or a loved one, is wet, whacky, and wobbly, don't rest until you get answers that make all the pieces of the puzzle fit.

And the last take away? This getting old stuff isn't for sissies.

6

SHOWIN' THE PLAN

B elieve it or not, I've been blogging for nearly a year. Why is that surprising? Because my output is pathetically limited; I've so few posts to show for it. I've come to believe that my work is measured not by words per minute but rather hours per word. I think it was somewhere in *A Moveable Feast* that Hemingway described his efforts, at times, to be like "chiseling through granite with a toothpick." I feel his pain.

Which, of course, brings us to the topic of self-help books. I've read my share in my time. Almost all of them in my Amway days back in the early nineties. I got in hook, line, and sinker. My wife, in short order, jumped in the deep end with me. And believe me we read plenty of self-help books.

We listened to even more Amway tapes from Diamond producers and drove to twice monthly in-town, open meetings to hotels around town. (If you know what you're looking for, you can see notices of these meetings if you happen to be at the right hotel on the right night.)

Four times a year we drove to gigantic rallies with thousands of distributors from Orlando to Sacramento and many cities in between. We would leave Denver Thursday after work and drive all night to make it in time for the Friday night start of a frenetic "Dream Weekend" that would run into the wee hours of Saturday morning and then and do it again Saturday night. We would then climb back in the car on Sunday around noon, after a church service that was part of the weekend, and book it back to Denver, arriving in the wee hours of Monday morning—all while trying to steer clear of the of the 2 a.m. hallucinations on I-70 in Kansas willing the glow of Denver to appear in the western sky. We would arrive home with just enough time to fall into bed for a few hours of sleep before staggering, bleary eyed, into work.

It wasn't uncommon to hear accounts on the tapes of distributors getting into car wrecks; it's only surprising there weren't more. One in particular stands out.

He was a "tough as old shoe leather" dairy farmer who said he got in the business because he was "sick and tired of being sick and tired of his blue john existence." When he woke up from the wreck, "the wheel was wrapped around the steering column." And his growl implied, if you're not tough enough to do it yourself, you're a sissy.

Over the course of those four or so years, we talked to hundreds of people about Amway. Very few joined us. And those who did, didn't stick around for long. Far from making money, especially the much vaunted residual income, we lost money. True, it wasn't much. But at that point, with three little kids, we didn't have much to spare.

The worst thing about the business for me was that it was like pouring gas on my bipolar disorder. Bipolar thrives on a variety of things, including inadequate sleep, stress, and financial worry. The rally-induced highs of the business were stratospheric. The rejection-induced lows of the business were stygian. Of these, the business provided a great abundance.

In retrospect, I'm very grateful for one thing about our Amway experience: it didn't kill us. Either in a car wreck or me with suicide; believe me, I thought about it more than once. The thought of missing out on seeing our kids—and now grandkids—grow into the wonderful people they've become is . . .

Is it *possible* to strike it rich in Amway? Of course. It's a multi-billion-dollar, international business. *Someone's* got to be making money. It just wasn't us.

The turning point for me came one summer at a Free Enterprise super rally at the sixty-thousand-plus domed stadium in Indianapolis. Worked into a frenzy by speaker after speaker, the SRO crowd delighted in launching one raucous wave after another around the coliseum; I enthusiastically joined in.

But then it came time for the new "pins" to go across the stage. These were couples that had reached a higher, more lucrative level in the business. There weren't many. And of the high-level pins, like diamonds, you could count them on one hand. Out of a crowd of tens of thousands. I very clearly remember thinking, "We have a better chance of winning a gold medal in the Olympics than making it big in this business."

So we quit. But it's a funny business. Almost like malaria, it's very unpleasant, and once it's in your blood, it's almost impossible to entirely shake. Over the years, I've occasionally googled some of my big "up line" diamonds—can't seem to help myself. Like all of us, their stories are a mixed bag. Some are doing fine. Some are not. With others, it's pretty ugly, their feet of clay in full view.

But did it make us stronger? Not sure. But I will give it this: it didn't kill us.

7

THERE ARE UNQUIET MINDS

AND SLIGHTLY LESS UNQUIET MINDS

Steve Kinsky is an old friend. We first met when we were both in a professional organization for health insurance agents. We've stayed in touch since we retired. We're both widely read, although our tastes sometimes differ since Steve has a scientific and mathematical bent that I don't share. Before becoming an agent, he was an actuary.

Steve's known for some time that I have bipolar disorder; I'm not quite sure how he learned about it. He may have read about it in this prior post of mine. Anyhow, he came to know, and we've discussed it more than once.

Last time we met, he suggested that I take a look at a book he'd recently read about bipolar called *An Unquiet Mind: A Memoir of Moods and Madness* by Kay Redfield Jamison. Published in 1997, the book is beautifully written and makes compelling reading.

RACING DOWN THE HALLWAY NAKED

Like most illnesses, bipolar comes in a variety of shapes and sizes. Or, to state it more precisely, it comes with varying levels of intensity. In my case, it was relatively mild. But that doesn't mean that I wasn't involuntarily committed to a psychiatric hospital as a young adult. Or that I didn't have wild mood swings between manic, sleepless highs and lows that left me carefully planning my own destruction. Rather, it means that I never, as my psychiatrist once told me of other cases he knew of, ran naked down the hallway of a psychiatric hospital screaming at the top of my voice.

Judging from Jamison's book, my guess is that her disorder is of the more severe variety. While she's a brilliant author and clinical psychologist who specializes in this illness, she's gone beyond the planning stage and actually attempted suicide. She's also gone on the wild spending sprees that are typical of the disorder. I, on the other hand, only *suggested* to my business partner the completely inappropriate purchase of luxury cars to "prove" how successful we were. He immediately, and fortunately, scotched the idea.

In short, while I've had more than enough near misses to make the lives of my family and me plenty miserable at times, Jamison was on an emotional roller coaster that continued unremittingly for years at a time.

THE AGONY AND THE ECSTASY

Jamison describes her experience with bipolar as a love-hate relationship. That's fitting. As is typical for this condition, I resisted taking medication for literally decades after I was first diagnosed. Why? Pride. Denial. A belief that my conversion to Christianity would make medication unnecessary. They all played a part, as they did to one degree or another in Jamison's life.

Bipolar's the sort of illness that one can become attached to. Jamison writes about it. I've felt it. The seemingly inexhaustible energy. The perceived brilliance of mind. Even now, years after the condition has been well controlled by medication, I occasionally feel a wistful fondness for those exhilarating times of mental acuity. Until, that is, I recall the inevitable and crushing lows that follow the euphoria.

It's estimated that 2.3 million Americans, or nearly 1% of the population, are bipolar. Suicide is the number one cause of premature death among people with the disorder, with 15% to 17% taking their own lives. Those aren't good odds. If you suspect that a loved one, or you, are wrestling with an unquiet mind, figure out a way to get help.

8

WHAT'S NORMAL GOT TO DO
WITH IT?

HOLE IN OUR HEADS OR IN OUR HEARTS?

Why they call it *normal* pressure hydrocephalus entirely escapes me. There's nothing normal about it. For obvious reasons, however, the condition's name has been shortened to NPH.

The cause of the condition escapes me. But here I'm joined by the entire medical-scientific complex. Absent some other trauma to the brain, it just seems "to happen" to a few old folks like me.

But what NPH does to those whom it afflicts is pretty well known: excess spinal fluid accumulates in your skull which then "squeezes" the brain. The symptoms that often follow are also pretty well known: wet, wacky, and wobbly. I've written about this dandy little condition before, in April of 2017. The condition is usually progressive. So, what's new with me over the last two and a half years?

WET?

Urinary incontinence. Now, there's a fun one. I could tell you stories about my days campaigning door to door, far from any public bathroom, that you probably don't want to hear. Or what it's like to get home and do my best to change my clothes and take a shower before anyone sees me, or my pants. But I'll spare you those as well.

But here I definitely have good news. Several years ago, after I *finally* got an accurate diagnosis, they put another hole in my head, installed a brain shunt, and began draining excess fluid from my head to my abdominal cavity where my body cleanses it before returning it to my skull. With the shunt at work, the progression of the "wet" condition has slowed markedly—if not completely. But not, as I hoped—and as sometimes happens—reversed.

WACKY?

Wacky? Yes. But far more than mere weirdness, which is a largely self-inflicted malady of youth—these days, millennials. It's one of the most feared diagnoses of the elderly (aside from being "elderly" itself): Dementia. Forgetfulness. Memory loss. Trouble dealing with routine tasks.

What's changed in my mental acuity during these years? Hard to say for sure. Is that a good sign, an indication that the changes, if any, are so subtle that I can't even put a finger on them? Or a bad sign, that my memory is failing? I can't really say for sure.

I do take some comfort, however, in this blog. If nothing else, it's a strenuous mental workout. It forces me to stay informed and, I hope, to communicate clearly. Now, if I can just get enough people to confirm that opinion by following this blog, I'll be in like Flynn.

WOBBLY?

The third one? The good news is that it isn't embarrassing. The bad news? It's scary in a physical, rather than mental, sort of way.

In the literature it's called "gait disturbances." But I liken it to being on the deck of a ship in a storm. I tell myself that most people probably don't notice me wobbling down the sidewalk as if I'd have trouble passing a roadside sobriety test. And no one has ever said anything about it. But nevertheless, the formerly simple act of stepping off the curb is an adventure. Moreover, if I can possibly avoid it, I never go down stairs without a firm grip on the handrail.

I do my best to stay active. I almost invariably park my car at the far end of the parking lot and walk to the front door of the store. Twice a week I work out with a trainer who focuses on agility and strength. For an additional three to four more days a week I work out on an elliptical and lift weights. So, for my age, I'm in pretty good shape. But mind over matter isn't a breeze when the mind that controls the matter refuses to fire on all cylinders.

THIS GETTING OLD STUFF ISN'T FOR SISSIES

When I was a kid, there was a song that made a brief appearance on the charts of Denver's ultra-cool Top 40 AM radio station, KIMN. It was "Those Were the Days." Not sure why a Lithuanian folk song reached the top of the charts for teenagers, but it made an impression on me.

And now, pushing seventy, with my share of the medical slings and arrows that come with advanced age, it's more than just a catchy lyric:

> Those were the days my friend
> We thought they'd never end

We'd sing and dance forever and a day
We'd live the life we choose
We'd fight and never lose
For we were young and sure to have our way.

There are probably about as many ways to interpret this tune as there are people who hear it. But it reminds me, as seventeenth-century French inventor, mathematician and theologian Blaise Pascal once wrote, there is a "God-shaped hole in the heart of each man that can only be satisfied by God, made known by Jesus Christ."

"Those Were the Days" and Pascal were talking about the same thing. The nagging fear, even if we can often suppress it with mindless diversions, that this life won't be all that we hoped for. That, in the end, we might not get our way. And that, the relentless march of time will get us in the end. Unless, that is, we can bring ourselves to allow the Great Physician to mend our broken hearts—and heads—as only he can.

9

YOU GOTTA BE CRAZY

S everal years back, I tried to purchase a new shot gun. Don't remember exactly why. Maybe because the old Remington 1100 that Dad had given me as a Christmas gift decades earlier was getting lonely in my flimsy gun safe.

Whatever. I jumped on I-25 and drove south to the Cabela's super store perched on the slope of a bluff overlooking Denver in all its rapidly metastasizing glory.

Having made my decision on a gun with a salesman, he led me to a computer that automatically administers background checks to determine who's fit to purchase a firearm. I was grateful he didn't stick around to look over my shoulder as I went through the questionnaire.

The first few questions were softballs. But when I got to the one that read "Have you ever been adjudicated a mental defective or committed to a mental institution?" I hesitated. Yes, I'd been committed to a mental institution. But that had been decades before, probably 1973. Would the state's records even go that far back? If I answered yes, would I have the opportunity to talk to someone in the store about my case? What if I simply lied and answered no?

It didn't take long to decide to stick to the truth. I didn't know for sure but was pretty confident that a lie would set me up for a felony charge, which, at best, would mean a protracted, embarrassing, and expensive legal fight and, at worst, a prison sentence.

Not to mention the most obvious consideration: I would be lying.

So, I clicked the yes button. Instantly, the screen went blank, and I was directed back to the counter where I'd left the gun with the clerk. Sheepishly I said, "I was denied at the computer. What do I do now?"

"I'm sorry," he answered as he locked the gun in the glass case behind the counter. Although he acted as if my problem was an everyday thing for him, he went on, "There's nothing we can do here. You'll have to go to the Colorado Bureau of Investigation. Maybe talk to an attorney. Or," he continued, "join Legal Shield." He handed me a card. "They might be able to help."

TO BUY A GUN

A few days later I was in the office of an attorney who was part of Legal Shield, a prepaid plan for gun owners. Don't remember his name; he probably wasn't glad to see me. Prepaid plans like that stir up a great deal more chaff than wheat. And I was definitely in the chaff category. But the quick discussion convinced me that my next stop should be the Denver Probate Court, the entity that would have made the determination that I should be committed to Mount Airy Psychiatric hospital.

It'd been years since I'd been in the Denver City and County Building. But the broad hallways with the little clusters of worried people huddled around their attorneys outside courtrooms were the same. I wondered around some before I found the probate court. Its filing room smelled like old dust.

The bulky, pasty-faced clerk, who looked like he'd been there as long as the dust, asked, "Can I help you?"

"Yes, thanks," I said. "My parents had me involuntarily committed to the Mount Airy Psychiatric hospital back in the early to mid-seventies. Can you show me how to find my file?" No sense beating around the bush with a probate court clerk; they must see commitments like this all the time.

"Sure," he answered, leading me to a bank of filing cabinets. "The index is organized by year and then last name of the respondent, which in this case would be you. What's your name and what year did you say?"

"It's Swalm," I said before spelling it out. "Early to mid-seventies."

"Ok," he said, stooping over and pulling out a bank of index cards. "This is for 1970. It continues here for '71 and goes on here," he said, pointing.

"Thanks," I said as he walked away. I began fingering my way through the cards. Nothing for 1970. Or 1971.

Or, to my surprise, '72, which was the most likely year. I was pretty sure that was the year I took a break from CU Boulder to write the great American novel. And the year I endured another nasty breakup with Lolly, which, in my despair, drove me to Christ.

But nothing of the wild whipsaws of that year showed up in the probate court records. Or for '73 or '74 or '75 or '76. I gave up and concluded that the record wasn't there. I even went back a second time a few weeks later just to make sure. Nada.

Could it have been a figment of my imagination?

But the two Denver sheriffs who escorted me out of my folks' basement, put me in the back of their patrol car, and drove me to Mount Airy weren't a figment of my imagination. Nor was the soft-spoken teenage girl at Mount Airy who washed her hands so much that they bled. Neither was Dr. Walker, my psychiatrist, who ordered the anti-psychotic Mellarill without telling me it caused constipation. An omission which caused my mania to bubble to the surface in an angry outburst toward him. Or the girl, a little older than the hand washer, whose distended belly held the child that was destined to be aborted. Or her boyfriend that visited her in the evening, somehow banging her in the bathroom, while their buddies stood guard. Or the court appointed attorney with whom I talked to get him ready to represent me in the hearing I'd demanded to challenge the commitment, the commitment my parents had requested because a pheasant hunting trip with Dad had gone sideways. Badly.

All that had happened. I was sure of that. Even if the court file had vanished.

But what did happen to it? Could it have just slipped into a crack somewhere? There are plenty of cracks for what would have been a slender file to hide in a room full of hundreds, no thousands, of files. Since that's the simplest answer, it's probably the right one.

But that's not the answer that appeals to me.

My dad, Paul, was a Denver City Councilman. Before that, he'd served a two-year term in the Colorado House of Representatives. At one point, before us kids talked him out of it because of his history of heart attacks, he seriously considered running for governor of the State of Colorado. From abject poverty as a child, he built multi-million-dollar businesses. Along the way, he'd survived polio, tuberculosis, rheumatic fever, whooping cough, and small pox. A smart, tough, hardworking guy, he didn't tolerate obstacles gladly.

Was a guy like that going to let a crazy son like me cast a potential shadow over whatever he might want to achieve? I don't think so.

So how tough would it have been for him, the city councilman, or state representative, or the gubernatorial candidate— or whatever—to saunter into the probate court, talk to some lowly clerk, and make that file go away? Or, if that was too risky, hire someone to do it for him? Probably not too tough.

And was I, the crazy son, going to object to having my past wiped clean? Why would I? It was decades before I was willing to talk about Mount Airy with anyone other than my wife.

So what do I do now? Jump through a bunch of bureaucratic hoops to try to fix my record just so I can buy a gun? And maybe even be forced to testify, under oath, that I was never committed under a mental health hold?

You gotta be crazy.

10

IF

My partner in the insurance business was a man named Tony Cook. Smart, unflappable and with a gentle sense of humor, he came to insurance by a circuitous route, like me. His route, however, was more so than mine. Tony came from a military family; he'd served as a French interpreter during the Vietnam war. He taught French after the war at Denver University back when it teetered on the edge of bank-ruptcy. Tony robbed the cradle at DU, marrying one of his lovely students, Carolyn. Teaching French was an occupation that allowed him, as he put it, "to live in gentile poverty." But it didn't allow for a family; hence, the switch to insurance.

Tony's father, Charles, graduated from Annapolis in time to get into the thick of it in the Pacific during World War II.

During the furious sea battles off the tiny island of Guadal-canal in the early days of the war, Charles was a junior officer working in the bowels of the cruiser USS *Helena*. The *Helena*'s first engagement off Guadalcanal was a chaotic nighttime encounter, the battle of Cape Esperance. Although the *Helena* survived Cape Esperance unscathed, she was later torpedoed and sunk near the end of the brutal six-month fight for the island, which ended with a Japanese defeat in February of '43. Tony's dad was among the thousand survivors.

Charles did more than simply live to raise a family after the inferno of WWII. He also lived to tell the tale in his book, *The Battle of Cape Esperance: Encounter At Guadalcanal.* "The fog of war" might be a hackneyed phrase when it comes to battles. But that doesn't make it any less true. And it applies in spades to what happened on the night of October 11, 1942, off Cape Esperance. The Japanese navy was skilled at night fighting. (They didn't have much choice since they didn't have radar.) The Americans had radar on that night, but it was a new technology that they had yet to master. The result was utter confusion when the two sides blindly stumbled into one another and began firing at 11:46 p.m. off the Cape.

By the time it was all over the next afternoon, the Americans could claim victory. Not only because they had sunk more enemy ships, but mainly because they had learned enough hard lessons to demonstrate that they could go toe to toe with the Imperial navy that only two months before had dealt the American navy its worst defeat ever at the Battle of Savo Island as the see-saw struggle for Guadalcanal was just getting underway.

"If" is the name the then retired Captain Cook gives to the final chapter of his book. It's a series of speculations about how the battle's outcome could have been reversed had a number of seemingly small incidents gone differently.

Decades later, Tony and I occasionally visited in the insurance office at the end of the workday as he puffed on a cigarillo. I knew that Tony had a child that was battling bipolar disorder. In the throes of yet another debilitating bout with depression myself, I was finally willing to concede I needed help. Gingerly, I approached Tony with the subject. "I was committed to Mount Airy Psychiatric Hospital years ago. The highs and lows of bipolar are something I've struggled with occasionally ever since. Have you found a psychiatrist who's helpful?"

"Yes," Tony responded, looking at me under a raised eyebrow. "Jay Carlson is very good. Let me give you his number."

Marleen and I were in Dr. Carlson's office before the week was out. It took time, but Dr. Carlson eventually figured out the right combination of drugs that smoothed out the wild highs and crushing lows that beset my mind.

Bipolar disorder wages war with little mercy. Researchers estimate that 25% to 65% of people with bipolar will attempt suicide. Four to 19% will be "successful," a rate that is substantially higher for men than women. Bipolar reduces the life expectancy of an average sufferer by nine to twenty years.

If Charles had gone down with the *Helena* during those desperate days off Guadalcanal so long ago, I'd never have met Tony, the son he never would have had. And I probably wouldn't have met Dr. Carlson.

If I hadn't met Dr. Carlson, would I have committed suicide? It's not idle speculation; more than once I methodically plotted how to do myself in.

But in the end, I'd answer, "No, I probably wouldn't have killed myself." With Shakespeare, I believe "There is a tide in the affairs of men." And the tide is called God.

Of the precise reason why I was spared, I'm less certain. Is it because of the three wonderful children and now five beautiful grandkids with which I've been blessed? Not completely sure. But I'm confident that the world would be a poorer place without them.

11

WHOLE LOTTA SHAKIN' GOIN' ON

I t's not uncommon for me to go for a short walk before I closet myself in the upstairs bedroom and sit down in front of the computer keyboard. Anything to delay the inevitable. A few mornings ago, while making my rounds, I snitched on the owner of the home just outside my window to the north.

It's a rental house; we don't even know who owns it. The renters recently moved out and now the home is for sale. The large tree in the backyard is nearly dead. Once a majestic red maple, there are only a handful of sickly yellow leaves emerging at the very top. My wife and I eyed the tree nervously the other night as we sat on the back patio for dinner, wondering if the trunk might be rotten and a puff of wind could send it crashing down on our roof.

My wife confessed, "I've tried to get the attention of people looking at the house, so I could tell them that tree is dead and that the current owner should pay to have it cut down. But no luck yet."

There's a small office for our homeowners' association just around the corner that I walk by almost every day. The other morning, for the first time in memory, the door was opened, so

I poked my head in, maintaining the appropriate social distance.

"Hi," I said to the woman behind the desk. "I'm Spencer Swalm. I know I recognize you, but I'm sorry, I don't remember your name."

"It's Katie," she said from behind her mask. "Our daughters were friends in high school. Good to see you again. How can I help you?"

"We live over on South Ivy Court. The house on the corner, just to our north, recently went on the market. They have a large tree in the backyard that's dead. We're concerned that it might fall on our house if a wind comes up. Is that something the homeowners' association handles?"

"Yes," she replied as she handed me a form. "Fill this out and leave it with me."

As I returned the completed form, I asked, "Is there anything else I need to do? Will we hear from you?"

"No," she said. "That's all; we'll take it from here. And you won't hear from us."

Back in front of my keyboard, I looked out the window that faces to the east. There, I saw our maple tree full of leaves. At the ends of supple new shoots, its tender green leaves gracefully swayed and danced in the breeze.

To my left, the brittle branches of our neighbor's dying tree shuddered arthritically in the same breeze.

I take a couple of medications to keep my bipolar disorder in check: depakote and risperidone. Both these anti-psychotic drugs, not surprisingly, have side effects. Among them are the shuddering tremors that cause me to occasionally drop a piece of food in my lap in the split seconds it takes my fork to go from my plate to my mouth. (I take a third drug, metoprolol, to help dampen the shakes.) Losing a piece of food from your trembling fork before it can make it to your mouth isn't as damaging as having a tree come down on your roof—unless, of course, you're talking about injured pride. Do I like the side effects of the medications I take? No. But when compared with the real-world consequences of unchecked bipolar disorder, the choice is obvious. Been there. Done that.

THE COCK CROWS, SO THE SUN RISES?

A lot's changed since April 2005. I can't ski any longer; my brain, afflicted with normal pressure hydrocephalus (NPH), has seen to that. We don't own a share of a condo in Vail anymore. My eight-year term in the Colorado House of Representatives has come and gone.

But the traffic on I-70, especially on weekends, remains an infuriating constant for folks headed to Colorado's high country on weekends. But now that traffic is even spilling over to the "shoulders" of the weekends: Thursday afternoons all the way to Monday afternoons.

Aren't you glad all those Colorado boosters at our chambers of commerce have done such a fabulous job attracting those hordes by singing the siren song of our state's wonders? Call me a curmudgeon, but I'm emphatically *not* glad. But that's for another post.

Back in April 2005, we drove up I-70 on a Friday afternoon for a weekend at our Vail condo and some spring skiing. The traffic was insane. Under fair, warm skies, for some reason it had come to a near standstill east of Georgetown. Why? Several unbearable miles later, we saw that a few of our state critters, Rocky Mountain Big Horn Sheep, had parked themselves on the shoulder of the road and were licking the salt residue left by sanding crews battling ice during the previous winter. Of course, everyone had to slow down to see the creatures.

SOMEBODY OUGHTA DO SOMETHING

My blood boiled. And, with not much else to do in the stop-and-go jam, my mind raced: "What can be done to fix this every-weekend nightmare?" The question had particular significance for me because I'd already begun thinking about becoming the Republican candidate for state House District 37 in the upcoming election. "What better way to get elected than to figure out a way to straighten out this mess?" I asked myself.

Three things occurred to me. One, put up fences to keep the animals away from traffic like there are along many other stretches of I-70 in the mountains. Out of sight, out of mind. Two, make the road lousy with state patrol to reign in the reckless drivers who cause the wrecks that plug up the narrow corridor for hours. And have tow trucks prepositioned along the road to clean up the inevitable crashes as quickly as possible. And three, add tolled lanes that could pay for themselves and better manage the high volume of traffic.

THE PEN IS MIGHTIER

Honestly, I don't remember much about what our family did that weekend. If I skied, it was probably near the last time; you try skiing when merely walking down a staircase—with a handrail, mind you—feels like an extreme sport. But I do remember sitting at the breakfast table writing—for hours. No doubt I occasionally looked up at the Gore Range to the east. But even that spectacular view was nowhere near enough to take me away from my monomaniacal focus. The article that laid out my solutions for I-70 traffic jams eventually appeared in the April 15, 2005, edition of the *Denver Business Journal*. I have a copy to this day. But don't even bother to hunt for it online; I did and it's long gone.

I can, however, claim that my suggestion for tolled lanes has either been adopted or is in the works. But, trust me, my little article from so long ago was not why the sun rose on those lanes.

TOLL ROAD MANIA

So, the real takeaway from that weekend? I was probably in the midst of a Type I bipolar manic break, which includes both highs and lows (as opposed to Type II, which is only the lows). And boy were both of those old friends to me. A bunch of the classic symptoms were there that weekend:

- Sleeplessness: Can I actually remember how much I slept that weekend? No. But I'd be willing to bet that the night before I sat down to write, the ideas rattled around in my head over and over as sleep refused to come. And the next night, the finished article replayed again and again as I tossed and turned.
- Abnormally upbeat and wired: House District 37? A piece of cake. Why not governor or US senator?
- Exaggerated sense of well-being and euphoria: Watch out world. Outta my way!

IT'S ALL DOWN HILL FROM HERE

The drive back down to Denver on Sunday was, predictably, very much like the drive up: maddeningly slow. How could it be otherwise?

But just as predictable? The other side of my Type I mania:

depression. Exactly when and what form did it take? I don't remember; they tended to run together after a while. But just like sun set follows sun rise, it came. Count on it.

IS THIS AMWAY?

There. The worst is behind me. Five years. At least. Not much more you can do to hurt me once you know that. Like a loose tooth that needs pulling or a Band-Aid that has to come off, it's best to get it over quickly.

It's a funny business. A rinky-dink soap business according to most. But with five years in and countless books, tapes, and rallies all over the country, I know better. The business isn't rinky-dink. It's more like it's just too tough for most people. Me included. But there's almost no one who wouldn't want to have the financial freedom it can produce if you have what it takes to build it big: A DREAM.

THE POINTY HEADED INSURANCE GUY—AND VIETNAM VET.

While we were in Amway, I was also an insurance salesman. My partner in that business was a guy named Tony Cook. I've mentioned him before. A Princeton grad, he was a French professor at Denver University before he got into insurance. And before he did that, he *volunteered* with the Army as a French interpreter in Vietnam. Six months after he came home in September '71, the province in which he had worked was overrun by the North Vietnamese. The closest a Princeton student gets to combat now? Screaming obscenities at a BLM riot.

Tall and lanky, Tony was an intellectual's intellectual. He wore used penny loafers that were so narrow they looked like short skis at the ends of his pipe cleaner legs. We were both avid readers, but Tony devoured esoteric books in English *and* French.

We were also classical music buffs, but my tastes weren't up to his rarified standards. "Colorado Public Radio plays the same music over and over," he told me once. With the passing of years and my continued listening to CPR, I can confirm that Tony pretty much nailed it: the station has something approximating a Top 40 list of the classical pieces. Of what else might be out there in the way of classical music, I'm a poor judge. But Tony was a good one; he must have had a huge record collection.

WHAT *DOES* IT TAKE?

Once, we went to meet with an insurance prospect on South Colorado Boulevard. I don't remember much about the meeting; I'd be surprised if we made the sale. But I knew that there was a Cadillac dealership we could drop by on the way back to the office. "Hey," I said to him, "why don't we stop in at Rickenbaugh Cadillac before we go back to the office?"

"Why would we want to do that?" responded Tony, looking at me skeptically from behind the wheel of the Mercury minivan that was the perfectly sensible choice for his family of five.

What he didn't know was that I was doing Amway on the side. "Well," I answered, "we need to have a reason to keep beating our heads against the wall of this insurance stuff, don't we? Wouldn't a nice car be a motivation?"

"I don't suppose," he answered, "that it would hurt if we stopped by for a few minutes."

So that's what we did. For a few minutes. I think Tony was clueless as to what I was up to. As unobtrusively as possible, he looked at the shiny objects on the showroom floor while fending off the circling sales sharks. While I did my best to conjure up a dream big enough to build Amway to the point where I didn't need to work for Tony any longer. While also fending off the salesmen. Oh, what a tangled web . . .

That stab at dream building didn't work then. Or any of the other many times I tried it. But the exhausting drives to frenzied "major functions" all over the country, from Orlando to Sacramento, were more than enough to trigger manic episodes.

RELEASE THE KRAKEN!

The self-contempt I could experience after yet another failed attempt to "show the plan" knew few bounds. Pound the steering wheel? You bet. Carefully plot how to get a revolver, hike up above the 4th of July campground toward Arapahoe Pass-a gorgeous valley that I knew so well-and veer off the trail into the thick woods and end it all under an obscure tree? Not to be found before some hunters happened on my rotting corpse during the next elk season? Yep. Been there. But, by God's grace, *didn't* do that. Curse myself in the vilest of terms? Again, yep.

But you'd best plug your ears and send the kiddies out of the room: *"You syphilitic rectal refuse!"* Don't shoot the messenger; I'm just reporting. For me, the nightmares were always the other side of *the dream*. At least, that is, until the inevitable rebound. At which point I was lower than a snake belly in a wagon rut. Again.

THIS TIME, IT'S PERSONAL

Why did I take the Amway business so hard? It's a good question. And one for which I'm not sure I have a satisfactory answer.

When someone told me no in the insurance business, it could be frustrating. And there were times I badly needed the money. But suicidal? No. Maybe it was because, although I believed in the product enough to own insurance myself, I never saw it as a particularly attractive solution to life's problems. Want to get something from your health insurance policy? Get sick. Disability insurance? Get so badly injured you can't work. Life insurance? Die.

Sure, protection from all those bad things is important. But insuring those bad things doesn't somehow transform them into good things. They're still disasters. Nowhere near a *dream*.

In the end, it was probably a combination of things. The untreated bipolar disorder. The "burning the candle at both ends" that poured fuel on the bipolar fire. But perhaps the best way I can explain it is every time someone told me no, it was like having someone peel open my chest, peer contemptuously at the dreams I held dear, and sneer, "Amway? I'm not interested in *that*."

THIS IS THE END

I finally told Marleen that I couldn't do it anymore as we drove to a "seminar and rally" in Colorado Springs one Saturday. After years of effort, the only thing we could show for our work were losses that we could use to off-set some of my meager earnings in the insurance business.

"Babe, I just can't do this anymore," I told her. "It's just too depressing for me."

"Yeah," she shot back at me, "so what are we going to do?

Live on my part-time nurse's salary? I'm not going back to work full time and put our kids in day care."

An icy silence filled the car during the drive to and from the Springs. And that was only the beginning of a lengthy ice age in our marriage.

14

HIDING IN PLAIN SIGHT

Did you know that May in Colorado is Mental Health Awareness Month? Probably not. We members of the Colorado Legislature observed Mental Health Awareness Month every year when I served in the House. Did we do it by resolution or memorial? Don't ask me. I hardly understood the difference when I was down there for eight years. And you can be sure I don't remember the difference now. But I'm certain that the observance was marked by a great deal of speechifying. And, man, could those politicians talk.

THE GUY WHO *DIDN'T* SPEECHIFY

But one guy who you can be sure didn't talk? Me. Yep. The guy who'd been involuntarily committed to Denver's Mount Airy psychiatric hospital back in the mid-seventies. The same guy who was taking the anti-psychotics Depacote and Risperidone for bipolar disorder.

Yep, that guy was sitting on his hands on the side of the House chamber often scowling and listening impatiently. The guy who probably knew more about bipolar disorder from first-hand experience than almost all the other one hundred members of the Colorado House and the Senate. Especially given that only about 3% of the US population suffers from the condition.

Why Was *that* Guy Sitting on His Hands?

I suppose I could blame my wife, Marleen. Being the wife of a politician was never her idea of fun. It was something she endured.

One time, we were at the office of my psychiatrist, Jay Carlson, and he suggested that it might be helpful for other people with mental disorders if I went public. I responded, "I'd be fine with that." But Marleen was adamantly opposed. I never pushed it thereafter. She made plenty of sacrifices in other ways: often having me come home late at night when the legislature was in session, many dinners alone while I was out campaigning door to door, occasionally accompanying me to political events where she was always uncomfortable. The idea that of it becoming widely known that her politician-husband suffered from a mental disorder was simply a bridge too far for her.

GOING OUT ON A LIMB

Looking at it from my perspective might be even more telling. Did the idea of spilling the beans in front to the entire House of Representatives appeal to me? In a certain way, yes. It sounded heroic to be perceived as a person who'd overcome and achieved a few things in life despite being a whacko and then had the courage to publicly talk about a subject that is still so often perceived as taboo. But on the other hand, it'd be tempting to excuse my silence by saying "my wife made me do it." Or, more accurately, *not* do it.

But that's not the whole picture.

THAT'S MY PATIENT!

On another occasion, we were in Dr. Carlson's office shortly after the November elections. Jay told us that he'd been at an election night party with some friends and colleagues watching the returns come in. He'd been keeping an eye on the local legislative races as they scrolled across the bottom of the TV set.

After my name had come and gone—which didn't take more than about a blink of the eye—Jay turned to the rest of the room and announced, "My patient won his election." Of course, he didn't mention me by name.

And that kind of thing stroked my ego. To hear that my name had been on TV, however briefly, was enjoyable. To see my name in the paper once in a while over the course of the eight years I served was pretty neat. I have a bulging file folder of clippings in my desk to this day. To even see my name scroll across the old *Denver Post* building when I'd made some controversial remarks during a debate in the House was exhilarating. (That, by the way, was the *only* time my name made it into those bright lights.)

The bottom line is, I *liked* recognition. I had a niggling fear that going public with my mental disorder might put my political career at risk. And given the scurrilous nature of political campaigns these days, it's not difficult to imagine how my history with mental problems could have been used against me. At least that's what I told myself.

THE MAN *NOT* IN THE ARENA

So, here I am. Retired. No longer in Teddy Roosevelt's arena. Nothing to lose. Finally willing to make a clean breast of it. Admirable? Heroic? Hardly. But, perhaps, it's better to be late than never at all.

15

SPRINGS OF LIVING WATER

A bunch of my extended family got together at our little neighborhood pool the other day. The Colorado sun was bright and hot. The water cool and refreshing. It was a load of fun for all the little ones.

There were some very interesting and talented folks in attendance. It was the first time that many of us had even met one another. It was wonderful. They delivered Dominoes cheese pizzas. While by no means gourmet (more on that later), it was a hit among the tykes. And, generally, the appropriate social distancing recommendations were observed by all.

GOD BLESS US, EVERYONE

It's best, of course, to begin at the beginning. Which, when it comes to events like these, means my wife, Marleen. No detail escapes her well-organized, drill-sergeant-like mind. And it certainly didn't fail us this time. The food, the drinks, the paper plates, the napkins, the plastic silverware: check, check, and double-check. And did I mention the pool side chairs? It's

BYO at our pool because of COVID. Yeah, Marleen had that covered too.

THE MEDIA DARLING

This is going to drive my daughter, Lauren, nuts but I'm going to do it anyway. This, after all, is *my* blog.

My cousin Paul has a daughter, Carrie Baird. (Lauren thinks I'm obsessed with her. And exactly how is my cousin's daughter related to me? First cousin once removed? Second cousin? I'm clueless.) In any event, Carrie *is* something of a local—and even national—celebrity chef. She placed high on the recent series, *Top Chef Colorado*. With her longtime boyfriend, Blake (who also joined us poolside). She's been involved with several successful Denver metro restaurants. Blake's family runs a spooky Halloween-monster business out of Greeley; you have to see it to believe what they're up to.

We hadn't seen either of them in a long time, so it was great to catch up. And believe me, what the Dominoes cheese pizzas lacked in terms of gourmet, Carrie and Blake have it covered like a blanket at their restaurants.

IT'S ALL IN THE FAMILY

So much for Carrie and Blake. Now, on to my own family.

In order of seniority, our first daughter, Lauren. (Her older brother, Byron, lives in Omaha, is a techie for Google, and couldn't get away for a Monday morning dip in the pool. *You lose!*) Lauren's a great nurse at Children's Hospital. At least, until this COVID thing hit. Then, with three delightful little ones (all boys except two girls), she decided it just wasn't worth continuing to work just one day a week. But how do I describe Lauren? "A woman with a mind of her own," probably fits. And she rarely hesitates to share it with me.

The youngest of our brood is Jocelyn. Mother of two more

equally delightful little granddaughters. A great, freewheeling chef in her own right, she, like her sister, is a winsome Christian. And how do I describe Jocelyn? She can light up a room just by walking in; to know Jocelyn is to like her.

OH! I ALMOST FORGOT

Carrie's sister, Abby, was also poolside with her two little towhead daughters. The youngest (sorry, I can't remember her name) is about three months old and brings to mind Bibendum, the Michelin Man. My aunt Joyce would have had a field day pinching her cheeks.

Abby's husband, Parker, was busy and couldn't join us. Why? He's a resident at the CU med school. He's also half native Alaskan and full-on mountain man. Get this: he recently climbed Colorado's highest peak, Mount Elbert, *carrying* his mountain bike. He didn't carry it back down. Parker and Carrie plan to return to Alaska when he completes med school.

YEAH? SO WHAT?

Aren't we badly off track here? What's all this swimming and family stuff got to do with what you told us this blog was about? In other words, mental health?

It's long been recognized that a number of psychiatric disorders tend to run in families. In other words, there's probably a genetic component for illnesses like depression, bipolar disorder, ADHD, and schizophrenia.

Now, don't get me wrong. Just because there's one certified whack job in our family, me, it doesn't necessarily mean there are others in that same family. It just means that there's a better chance of having another one in our family than in the populace at large.

THE REFINER'S FIRE

*Warning! Viewer discretion advised. This post is about to get
religious and may not be suitable for all readers.*

One time, Jesus said, "If anyone wants to come after Me, he
must deny himself and take up his cross *daily* and follow Me."
(Luke 9:23 NASB, emphasis mine)

"Ugh!" you might say, "What's that doing here? Sure
doesn't sound much like family fun, splish-splashing at the
pool."

True, the pool has very little to do with Christ's words. But
family has a whole lot to do with them.

"And why's that?" you could reasonably ask.

Because family, rightly understood *and* practiced, is a
crucible. And a high pressure one at that. Am I the perfect
spouse? Obviously, no. And if you doubt that, just ask my
wife. And so it goes for all spouses. And, for that matter, all
kids.

"So," you might ask again, "why get married at all if, in the
end, you're just going to make each other miserable?"

The simple answer? Because marriage and family are the
first and most fundamental tools that God uses to teach us that
—SURPRISE!—there just *might* be someone in the world more
important than me, myself, and I. And it's where we begin to
learn what it means to take up our cross *daily* and die to self.

I'D LOVE TO STAY AND TALK , BUT I'M NOT GOING TO

Is there more to be said on this topic? Yeah, I think so. In fact,
try the whole Bible. Which is probably about the smartest
thing I've said all day. And you know what? It's best to quit
when you're ahead.

16

IT'S HARD TO FORGET THE THINGS
YOU DON'T WANT TO REMEMBER

M y recollection is that I dialed John's number in the alley across the Sixteenth Street Mall from Denver's art-deco Paramount Theater. It was a dangerous call. I was just merging onto the latest of the many ramps I'd gone up to yet another manic phase of my bipolar disorder.

Given that it happened over fifteen years ago, not long before I launched my campaign for Colorado's House District 37, my memory of details is sketchy. (Especially since I've gotten to the age when I can hide my own Easter eggs.)

But there are some things of which I'm confident: We were at the Paramount. (Wikipedia refreshed my memory by confirming that, indeed, the Paramount was the last of the Mohicans for downtown movie palaces. Which is not to say there are no other movie houses in downtown-there are. But by comparison with the elegance of the Paramount, they have all the aesthetic appeal of a shoe box.) I was at the theater for one of the monthly meetings of the Leadership Program of the Rockies. LPR is a sort of charm school for Republicans seeking elective office. I was in the class of 2005. In looking over the list of other participants, I still recognize many names, a number of them have gone on to bigger and better things in a wide range of fields.

LPR is the brainchild of Shari Williams. Bob Schaffer is chair of the board and a former member of the US Congress who actually *kept* his pledge to limit his time in the DC swamp.

SOMETHING'S HAPPENING HERE, AND YOU DON'T KNOW WHAT IT IS

Back to the goings on in the Paramount. Bob Schaffer greeted us and made some opening remarks. The substance of his comments? Don't have a clue. But for some reason they got me sufficiently agitated that I got up in the middle of his presentation and made my way down the cramped row of fold up, old-school movie seats, muttering "Excuse me. Pardon me. Sorry," over and over until I got to the aisle leading to the lobby.

When I got there, it was immediately evident that I wasn't the only one who needed a break; several clusters of LPRers were caucusing around the lobby already. No place to make an emergency phone call to my political mentor, John Andrews. And what a mentor to have. John was a speech writer for President Nixon but the only advisor who resigned in protest as the Watergate scandal brought Nixon down. He was the Republican nominee for Colorado governor in 1990, president of the Colorado Senate, and founder and president of Colorado's feisty and conservative political think tank The Independence Institute. And it goes on from there; John is tireless.

So I headed out to the warm spring day looking for a place to make the call. The mall itself? No go. Too noisy with the tourist hoards, office workers on lunch breaks, and the mall shuttle busses crawling back and forth.

ON THE ROAD WITH JACK KEROUAC?

So I ducked into a shady alley that, who knows, may have figured into Kerouac's frantic—even manic—accounts of his brief layovers in Denver that were depicted in his famous novel.

"John?" I said as he answered. "This is Spencer. I just stepped out of a meeting of the Leadership Program of the Rockies where Bob Schaffer was talking. You wouldn't believe what he was saying." From there, I rushed into an agitated, untested political rookie monologue impugning the reputation of one of the most admired Republican conservatives in the state.

It wasn't long before John brought me up short. "Spence," he said. "I don't know exactly what Bob said. But I do know this. If you keep acting this way, I can't support your candidacy."

What else was said makes no difference. I said goodbye, hung up, and stepped out of the alley into the sun beating down on the mall. I was gasping for air like a fish out of water.

But was that glimpse into the abyss enough to bring me to the point of trying to figure out what was really going on? And deal with it? No. Of course not.

There were still miles to go before I slept.

17

A TWO-LEGGED STOOL

This bipolar stuff is tricky, like walking a tightrope. Tip too far toward mania and you think you're happy dancing on cloud nine. Tip too far toward depression, and you're mired in Bunyan's Slough of Despond. In my experience, the higher you fly, the further you fall.

Now, if you pressed me, I suppose I could get all technical about bipolar. There's Type I and Type II. I'm certainly no shrink and the differences between the two can be confusing to a simple crazy guy like me. I just know that I've had have my highs and my lows. And mine is one of the two types. And not the other.

DELUSIONS OF GRANDEUR

I reckon I had my first bipolar break as a kid who'd taken a year off college at CU Boulder to write the great American novel.

Instead of buckling down and writing, what really happened was that I'd gotten involved in a tumultuous relationship with a woman named Lolly and was in way over my head. There were only two lasting results of that on-again, off-again train wreck of a romance. First, I got so depressed that it drove me to Christianity. Second, on the rebound from a particularly nasty bout with depression, I experienced my first go-round with mania. And what a doozy it was.

Walking over the footbridge to cross Boulder Creek on my way to Norlin Library, I nearly persuaded myself that I was Jesus Christ. (Ask yourself: "Would he lie about something as nutty as this?) I can still picture it. Leaning on the railing of the bridge, looking down into the dappled, swirling waters of the creek on that bright fall day, wondering *Is it possible?* "Hello, Spence. It's not!

From there, it was only a few days to the pheasant hunting trip with my dad in northeast Colorado where things got *really* ugly, and I persuaded myself that he wanted to kill me.

Again, you can't make this stuff up.

FORTY YEARS IN THE WILDERNESS

Sure, that's probably a bit of a stretcher. But not by much. There were years—even decades—when I had very little understanding of the demon with which I was wrestling. Sure, I'd been involuntarily committed to the Mount Airy Psychiatric Hospital after that hunting trip—and put on anti-psychotic meds. But when I was released, I immediately thought, "Who needs these pills? I've got Jesus." So I quit taking the pills.

Up and down. Up and down. Up and down. For years. Not always as bad as that first go-round. But sometimes they were. And when they were—especially on the down swing—they were dangerous. Like blow your brains out dangerous. With a lovely wife and three wonderful kids, makes me shudder even now.

THAT'S MY STORY. AND I'M STICKIN' TO IT

It must have during one of those nastier bouts with mania that Marleen spoke with her sister, Annie, about what was going on. Annie's a nurse too. She raised the possibility of bipolar. At least that's what I remember hearing somewhere along the way. Although when I recently called Annie to confirm my memory, she had no recollection of the conversation. Whatever. I'm stickin' to my story.

So Marleen and I went to see a shrink who had an office just around the corner. Grim? Ah, yes. Dark room. Dark Naugahyde upholstery. Curtains drawn. The guy peering down at us from behind a big desk like we were truant school kids. In a word? Creepville. His solution? Lithium.

We hadn't pulled out of the parking lot before Marleen said, "No way. I'm not going back there. And Lithium?" she went on, "that's strong stuff. I don't think you should be using it." And this from a woman who was a nurse. And who'd pretty much seen it all from me: the good, the bad, and the ugly.

So, I asked for a reference from my business partner, Tony Cook, who'd had some experience with a Dr. Jay Carlson, a psychiatrist who'd helped one of Tony's kids with some mental health issues.

"I'VE GOT TO ADMIT IT'S GETTING BETTER"

Carlson never mentioned Lithium. But Depakote? Check. Risperidone? Check again. Both are anti-psychotics. Both have potentially nasty side effects. But trust me, the disorder is worse than the any cure I've tried. And now, before I lay me down to sleep, I faithfully pop those pills.

We first met with Dr. Carlson ten, maybe twelve years ago. I'm sixty-nine now (in 2020). I was released from Mount Airy when I was about twenty-one. So more like thirty years—

rather than forty—with just Jesus as my co-pilot. Do I believe He could have healed me? Sure. But for whatever reason, He didn't.

In any event, there were finally two legs of the stool firmly in place: the Rock of Christ and those anti-psychotic meds.

HA! FOOLED YA!

Now, seriously, who's ever heard of a two-legged stool? Well, I guess Dilbert has. But other than that goofball? Only some seriously demented furniture makers.

But let's get real. A two-legged stool is about as useful as a screen door on a submarine.

So, the third leg for me? Family. No question. And, yes, there've been some bumps and bruises for them along the wild ride of my ups and downs. But could I have made it without them?

I won't even hazard a guess.

NATURE OR NURTURE?

O ur local rag—the *Denver Post*—ran a front-page story on September 3, 2020 with the headline, "Mental Health Issues Spike." (I tried to find the on-line version to link it here, but no dice. Why? Not sure. The *Post*'s internet pipeline is as shriveled as the paper's hard copy version?) Whatever.

The article describes the bulging caseloads of mental health therapists as they attempt to cope with the growing number of Americans who are depressed and anxious about what they're seeing every morning on the front page. And every night on their TV screens. COVID. Riots. Joblessness. An acrimonious election.

According to the article, the actual percentage of American adults suffering from depression? About fifty. And who can blame them? What's not to be depressed about?

FEEL. FELT. FOUND.

Back in our Amway days, we were members of the "Tape of the Week" club. I enjoyed them. Usually recordings of the good ol' southern boys who seemed to form the backbone of the business, they were often laugh-out-loud funny. And they almost always had some sales tips that sounded like they couldn't possibly fail to persuade a "prospect" to get into the business with us. At least, until those tips first encountered "the enemy," i.e., the prospect. At which point I experienced, over and over, the maxim, "No battle plan ever survives first contact with the enemy."

One line I was particularly taken with when trying to overcome an objection was, "I know how you feel. I felt the same way. But this is what I found out." No idea how many times I tried that. But I *can* tell you how many times it actually worked: zero.

Go ahead. Call me a slow learner. But we're not talking Amway here. We're talking depression. And I've certainly been more "successful" jousting with that than I ever was with Amway prospects.

THE WORST OF TIMES

For those of you who are depressed by all the stuff going on, I know how you feel. For the first several months after COVID slumped down on our heads like a wet blanket, I was nearly paralyzed. Especially, and most importantly, in terms of blogging. Sure, I could sit in front of the keyboard. And I could workout. I could go for walks. Reading? Sure. But productive writing? Not on your life. And the longer it went on, the worse it got. It was a vicious downward spiral.

BET YOUR BOTTOM DOLLAR THERE'LL BE SUN

When did it finally relent? Not really sure. But I do know that, come rain or shine, I sat down in front of that computer screen day after day. Even when nothing came. And eventually the gloom lifted. Even as the storm clouds beyond my office window got more threatening as spring rolled into summer.

And the probable, grim alternative to this small universe that my life had shrunk down to during those difficult days earlier this year? You guessed it: lots of TV. Talk about the cure being worse than the disease. Especially when you consider the steady diet of Frank Azar's "Strong Arm", commercials that make any extended stay in front of the tube almost inevitable.

I KNOW, I KNOW. I'VE GOT IT EASY

Now, I know my problems probably aren't as bad as yours. I'm retired. I have a secure income. The kids are grown, out of the house, and doing a good job of taking care of themselves. My wife and I generally get along well. No doubt, I'm blessed.

But are you bipolar like I am? Not likely. It afflicts a bit less than 3% of American adults. And I wouldn't wish it on anyone.

But it does have certain advantages over your garden variety depression. It's a pretty well recognized diagnosis. There are effective medications to treat it. And, at least in my case, after about ten years of wrestling with this demon I know the wisdom of "keeping your friends close, but your enemies closer." And that's what I've tried to do.

TAKE IT FROM ONE WHO KNOWS

Winston Churchill suffered from depression. He called it his Black Dog. I like that way of putting it. Ominous. Menacing. It's all that and more. When it begins nipping at your heels, either by nature (genetics) or nurture (environment), it's not to be trifled with. Suicide takes the lives of over 48,000 people a year in this country. And believe me, they're not killing themselves because they're happy.

Given all the tumult and uncertainty in the US at present, that's not a number likely to go down any time soon. So if the

Black Dog is stalking you, run don't walk to the nearest place where you can get some help.

19

LOVE YOUR NEIGHBOR? SURE. BUT YOURSELF? NOT SO FAST

Marleen and I meet with a few other members of our church, Greenwood Community, a couple of times a month. Actually, we Zoom, what with all this COVID stuff. Our small group is one of several at Greenwood who meet to discuss the Bible and encourage a greater sense of community at our relatively large church.

A meeting or two ago, and for reasons I can't put my finger on now, the discussion veered in the direction of the two Great Commands of Jesus. First, love God with all your heart, mind, soul, and strength. And second, love your neighbor as yourself.

Pretty straight forward, right? Make God numero uno. And your neighbor numero duo. Or something like that.

IF WE CAN'T DO IT, WHY COMMAND IT?

Now, it seems pretty clear that the first of those commands is just that: a command. Assuming that we have free will (which I do), it can either be obeyed or not. But, at least in my case, it's a command that is much more readily honored in the breach than in the observance. In fact, it's safe to say that I've *never* loved God perfectly. That is, with my whole heart, mind, soul, and strength. That's an impossibly high standard. And, in my book, the only person who's ever measured up is Christ himself.

"But why," you might ask, "would God command something that can't be done?"

Great question. Here's the simple answer: to demonstrate our need for the saving work of Christ on the cross.

SELF-LOVE? WHAT?!!!

But what about that second command? The one about loving your neighbor as yourself? For the longest time I believed that was just another command, very much like the first. And I think that's often how Christians view it. In other words, a command to love your neighbor. But what about the second half of that equation: love them *like yourself?*

Can we just *assume* that we'll love ourselves in such a way as to fulfill our duty to love our neighbor? I don't think so. In fact, when I raised this issue at our meeting the other night, at least one person thought I'd gone badly off the rails, asserting that loving ourselves was the opposite of what Christ was commanding.

And maybe he was right. It's not difficult to imagine self-love being twisted into an ugly, selfish parody of the second Great Command. But let's not throw the baby out with the bath water; Jesus did say that we should love our neighbor as we love ourselves.

AN UNBREAKABLE COMMAND

So, I've come to believe the Second Great Commandment is not a command that can be obeyed or ignored. It's more like a statement of the way things *are.* In other words, whether we want to or not, we *are* going to love or hate our neighbor very much like the way we love or hate ourselves.

"Right," you say, "now you're just talking in riddles. I love some people and hate others. Can I love and hate myself at the same time, all at once? Sorry, that's a square peg that doesn't fit in your round hole."

I have no beef with that. We can pick and choose when we're going to do what's right. And the same with what's wrong. And I do that sort of thing all the time. A friend I served with in the Colorado House was fond of quoting Ralph Waldo Emerson here: "A foolish consistency is the hobgoblin of little minds." So, when it comes to loving my neighbor—or not—no one would dare accuse me of having a little mind. And those two very different outcomes can vary virtually day to day, person to person, and issue to issue.

SO, WHERE'S THE BIPOLAR IN ALL THIS?

The wicked thing about bipolar is that it can put this "love yourself" thing on steroids. And the same with the flip side of that coin.

When I was in the throes of a manic phase, I didn't love myself. I *worshipped* myself. For days, even weeks at a time, I could persuade myself that I was the cock o' the walk, God's gift to the world. And if you didn't agree, there was hell to pay.

Like the time I got into it with Marleen about something—no clue what it was now and it doesn't matter—which ended with me tossing a plate, frisbee like, across the kitchen where it shattered at her feet. No, I don't remember what we were arguing about. But I can't forget the look on her face as the plate floated across the room.

By the same token, there was hell to pay on the down side. But I was the one who'd pay. I shudder to think how I thought of myself. How I plotted to snuff myself out. And this is how you love your neighbor as yourself? No. This is craziness pure and simple.

THERE ARE MASKS. AND THERE ARE MASKS.

Mention the need for masks in this season of COVID, and we all know where our thoughts turn. But before this bizarre era came down around our ears, mention masks and people thought of what? Halloween? Not sure.

But what about airplanes? You know the preflight routine where passengers are told to put on their own mask before assisting the kid next to them. And there's a good reason for it —like life and death.

Although Christ never flew in an airplane, I think that preflight monologue would have made sense to him. So, you want to get your mind right toward your neighbor? Start with getting your mind right toward yourself.

I HAVE TO ADMIT IT'S GETTING
BETTER

Take it from me, this bipolar thing can leave a jumbled pile of wreckage in its wake. For me, it's mostly about people: spouse, kids, relations, friends. But let's not forget the star of this little drama: me. Or, more specifically, the person suffering from the disorder. I didn't just *cause* the wreck. I got all tangled up right in the center of it.

REMEMBRANCE OF THINGS PAST

There's no way I remember—or will ever even know—all the heartache that this condition occasioned to those around me, and myself. Especially since—and this is one of my favorite gags—I've gotten to the age when I can hide my own Easter eggs. But even if I can't remember all of it, I know there's no shortage of heartache.

But there's one incident that has periodically come around in my memory, over and over like an old LP record with a scratch in it. (Is there anyone out there willing to show your age by admitting that you remember what LPs are?)

It's about a guy named Binker Blanchet—at least that's how I knew him so many years ago. His real name is Dave.

Although he's a year older than me, we were high school buddies.

WHAT COULDN'T HE DO?

When I think of Dave, the first thing that comes to mind is skiing. He was grace personified on the snow. The second? A dry sense of humor.

We shared a backpacking tent one night just below the Continental Divide in the Colorado Rockies. Between the bumps and the lumps, I couldn't get comfortable. "Man," I said in the dark, "this is an uncomfortable spot. I think I wound up on a rock."

"Here," he offered, "would you like to borrow my hiking boots for a pillow?"

We spent three summers during college working in Colorado ski resort towns. First, clearing trails during the early days of the Vail resort. Then two summers in Winter Park, just over Berthoud Pass from Denver on US 40. He worked for the US Forest Service. I dug ditches for Slim Manley.

After school, he joined the Forest Service in Alaska. I quit digging and didn't really know what to do next. Not long after Dave got to Anchorage, he climbed Denali-Mt McKinley, which at twenty thousand feet is the highest peak in North America. He invited me on that trip; I couldn't afford it.

At some point, he came to Denver to visit his mom. Not long before, his father had died in a horrific boating accident that occurred while he was in Alaska. While he was in town, Dave called suggesting that we get lunch. We met at a restaurant that was just around the corner from my law office near downtown.

FOOD POISONING

How the subject of abortion came up, I don't know. But I was probably the one who dragged it out; I was still militantly and self-righteously pro-life back then. Anyway, by the time we left the place, we were both so upset that I was convinced we'd probably never see one another again.

Except for that occasional, painful scratch on that part of my LP, nothing changed for decades. Until, without warning, that POP came around again this summer. And, for some reason, I decided to do something about it.

I googled him in Anchorage and sure enough David J Blanchet came up big as life. There was no phone number, but there was the address. So I resorted to that hideously outdated form of communication: pen and paper. I cast my bread on the waters. And just as Ecclesiastes says, it came back to me—but in the form of a twenty-first-century email.

DEATH WORKS BACKWARDS

Dave said he didn't even remember the argument. And that there was no cause to apologize. He sympathized with my struggles with bipolar, especially since he has suffered though bouts of depression himself. And to think I'd been held captive for years by bitter memories and fears.

We've exchanged several more emails, filling each other in on our families, what we'd been doing and such. I got the phone number of a friend in common that I'd lost track of decades before. A week or so later, when he'd returned from a mountaineering trip outside Anchorage, we spoke at length on the phone.

In his children's fantasy book, *The Lion, The Witch, and The Wardrobe* C.S. Lewis, the famous Christian author and Oxford don, describes Christ's sacrificial death and then resurrection as Death "working backwards."

I suppose that every act of reconciliation on a human scale is a repetition, writ small, of that divine act of reconciliation that was writ so large, so long ago. And I guess for me, that means that I no longer need to dread this particular scratch on my LP coming around again when I least expect it. At least death has worked backwards.

CUL-DE-SACS

I'm ashamed to admit how many times I've watched the Australian film *Unfinished Sky* over the last week or ten days. Actually, I suppose I could say that I have nothing to admit because I've completely lost track. Is it four or ten times? If I knew and fessed up, you probably wouldn't believe me anyway. Does the fact that it's a good movie make any difference? No. Or the fact for some of the showings I was grinding away on the elliptical? Again, no. There *are* better ways to spend your life.

And then, to add insult to injury, I binge watched the first two—and only—seasons of the BBC series Home Fires. Basically, it's a WWII soap opera that features the classic elements of the genre: melodrama, ensemble casts, and sentimentality. Yes, I was once more grinding away on the elliptical for a good bit of this treacly orgy. But so what? The show's still treacle.

ONE WAY OUT

So what gives? Well, one thing's for sure: I wasn't doing any writing during those many hours that I was parked in front of the tube. And after a while it wears you down. Big time. And the longer it went on, the further I sank. The classic reinforcing loop: once you get into it, there's the devil to pay to get out of it. Especially for someone like me who has the specter of bipolar disorder perched on my shoulder, always on the lookout for a way to insinuate itself back into the warp and weft of my life.

Back in the seventies, I lived in Boulder and got to know a guy named Dave Goodrich. We were both mountaineers, back country skiers, and rock climbers. But Dave worked in the basement of a music store on the Pearl Street Mall repairing guitars.

After all these years, he still has a shop on the mall. But he's now a well-known luthier, repairing fine stringed instruments for musicians of the Colorado Symphony and other orchestras.

Once in a while, I used to visit him in his subterranean digs near closing time. He always had the radio tuned to KBCO in the background. The DJ frequently played the Allman Brothers Band classic anthem One Way Out at about that time of day. I enjoyed it then. Still do on the rare occasions when I hear snatches of it now.

And the title of that song says a lot. Once I find myself in one of these blog post cul-de-sacs, it often feels like the only way out is the way I got in: start writing. And there's some truth to that. But at least in this instance it's not the whole truth.

LIFELINE

When it comes to this blog, I consider myself the brawn. The brain behind the brawn is a company called Orbit. They take the stuff I've written and with their internet wizardry get it out to the world. Andy Cleary is the head honcho over at Orbit. In this age of plague, I've never even met Andy face to face. True, I think we may have Zoomed once or twice. But Zoom, when you think about it, is a pitiful substitute for being able to shake someone's hand. Or, even better, give one of the grandkids a hug.

What made me think that Andy might be my lifeline out of this TV induced stupor? Not really sure, but whatever it was, the call I made to Andy finally got the rusted gears turning again. And what, precisely, did we talk about in our nearly hourlong conversation? *Gwaan!* Why would you ask me? Didn't you read my palsied memory gag?

I PICKED THE RIGHT FATHER . . . I GUESS

My dad was quite a guy. With a heck of a story.

His father, Wesley, was a church mouse poor religion professor at the tiny Nampa Nazarene College just west of Boise. Until, that is, he contracted tuberculosis and they moved him home to the frigid prairies north of Calgary, Canada, where they made him sleep in a tent.

Back in the early twenties, they believed cold was the cure for the lungs of those suffering from TB. And if cold was the ticket, Grandpa should have been as healthy as a horse. Instead, Wesley died. Dad was four or five. His sister, Alice, was about eight.

When what was left of the Swalm family got back to Nampa, the college offered my grandmother, Mable, a job cooking in the Beanery—the school's cafeteria. I suppose they considered it a sort of pension for her. But by whatever name, it was extremely meager.

Grandma couldn't afford to keep Dad on what she was making, so she arranged a sort of foster care for him with a family who went to her church. By the time he was thirteen or fourteen, Dad was effectively on his own.

He bounced around. He lumberjacked in the woods north

of Boise until he got to making too much money and the Wobblies drove him off. He got a job with Fluor Construction to build an airbase on Christmas Island in the South Pacific. On his way there, his ship laid over for a few days in Hawaii.

He was in a barracks overlooking Pearl Harbor on the night of December 6, 1941. The next morning, he was on the roof of the building watching ships of the US Pacific Fleet erupt in flames under a hail of Japanese bombs and torpedoes.

When he got back stateside, he volunteered for the military but was rejected; his right calf was shriveled from polio.

WE'RE IN THE MONEY

With the door to the military closed, Dad went back to working in the Idaho woods. That is, until someone showed him the Empire Crafts business. Empire Crafts was a multi-level marketing company whose products were china and silverware.

During the fifties, he became one of their most successful producers. His distributor organization probably numbered in the hundreds if not thousands. They stretched from Hawaii to Kansas and Oklahoma. He drove big Caddies. Flew tens of thousands of miles. Every year, he took his top producers to the white beaches of Waikiki. Near Christmas, he'd put our family on the Union Pacific Railroad for a ride to Ketchum, Idaho, where we skied the fabled slopes of Sun Valley.

Things were going great, that is, until the Japs struck again. Empire Crafts simply couldn't compete with the prices the Japanese charged for very similar products. So within the space of a year or two, Dad went from driving the Caddies with the big, outrageous tail fins to driving a used VW bug with oxidizing orange paint.

He had to start all over again, except this time in real estate —where he hit it even bigger. He sold hundreds of apartment units, industrial warehouses all over Denver, and an office building. He was a multi-millionaire.

From there? Politics: the Colorado House of Representatives. He was the last rock-ribbed conservative on the Denver City Council.

THE FLY IN THE OINTMENT?

There might be some in my family who contend that Dad was an alcoholic. Did he have a dry martini or two with an olive to unwind at the end of the day? Yes. Almost always. And on occasion he no doubt drank more than that. Did that make him an alcoholic? I'm not sure. But I am sure that if he was a drunk, he was a very high functioning drunk. And although he set high standards for us, he was never abusive to Mom or us kids. Was self-medication with alcohol his way of dealing with what was gnawing at his mind? Could that be what came to gnaw at mine? Don't know for sure. Probably never will.

He was also a terrific reader. At night, he would often park himself under the lamp at the end of the couch in the living room and read into the wee hours. But is insomnia the real name for his love of books? Again, I'm not sure. But I do know that during my manic phases, I could go for days with almost no sleep. Restless, mind racing, tossing and turning, yearning for the sleep that wouldn't come. Was that Dad too? Who knows. But there is a pattern.

I'm also confident that he struggled with depression. "Your dad used to come home from one of those trips for Empire Crafts so depressed sometimes," Mom told me once. "Another one of his salespeople had told him he was going to quit. It just killed him." Was this just garden variety disappointment? Certainly possible. But maybe it went deeper.

I do know, however, that I'm no stranger to depression. In fact, to serious bouts of depression. To bouts of depression which, with not much more than a nudge in the wrong direction, could have been life threatening.

So, what's all this got to do with me and my experience with bipolar?

Now, I'm no psychiatrist, but I've snooped around enough on the internet to know that a significant risk factor for bipolar disorder is heredity. In fact, the National Institutes of Health has published a study that says that genetic factors account for 60 to 80 percent of the cause of the disorder. So, in the final analysis my bipolar had to come from somewhere. And it seems that Dad, for all his other amazing talents and strengths, is about as good a suspect as I can come up with.

FROM THE DAY YOU'RE BORN, 'TIL
YOU'RE RIDING THE HEARSE

When I was just out of high school in 1970, I worked for a couple of summers digging ditches for a guy named Slim Manley. He had an ancient backhoe, a bulldozer, and a jack hammer. He dug ditches around the little town of Hideaway Park, a few miles west of the Winter Park Ski Area. The ski area is over the Continental Divide from Denver via Berthoud Pass on US 40. During the winter, the pass is subject to avalanches that can turn big trees into kindling, bury the road for hours, and occasionally sweep cars and their occupants over the edge of the highway and down the steep slope below.

Slim, who was even older than his equipment, knew what he was about. He ran the WW II surplus backhoe and the bulldozer. He surveyed the sewage lines that we dug to make sure they were on enough of a downhill grade that all the "stuff" that was in them got to the sewage treatment plant. He planted the dynamite charges in the "doneys" (high county lingo for "big boulders in the way of sewage and water lines" that needed to be blasted). Slim would worry away at those big rocks with that old backhoe until he was finally convinced that there was no choice but to blast. At that point I'd park myself on top of the doney with the jackhammer until there was a deep enough hole in the rock to plant the dynamite. Slim would take it from there, packing a stick of dynamite and a blasting cap into the hole with an old broom handle. The last step before the fireworks was to cover the boulder with an old mattress to, hopefully, keep rock splinters from going through the windows of the houses that often were no more than a few yards away.

Slim would attach extension wires to the blasting machine fitted with a plunger. We'd all retreat behind the bulldozer or into some other hidey hole. Slim would holler "fire in the hole," and there'd be a muffled "whomp." Except for the few times when there wasn't. In which case, rock splinters and dirt would come raining down. I don't remember any broken windows. But, then again, this was a long time ago.

HOMESPUN APHORISMS

To say that Slim had a dry sense of humor is an understatement. On one of those June days I worked for him, he showed up in the morning and announced, "Well, winter's on its way."

Of course, I was nonplussed. June 20 is the first day of summer! But the twentieth is also the summer solstice, the day on which days begin getting relentlessly shorter. And that meant something in a town set at about nine thousand feet above sea level where winter often held sway from shortly after Labor Day to Memorial Day. Where the surrounding peaks, at more than thirteen thousand feet, had snow fields on them year 'round, and could be dusted with new snow any month of the year. One of the traditions of Hideaway Park was the Fourth of July ski race on a snow field above town, just beneath the Continental Divide.

On another day—I was probably whining about something —Slim, without missing a beat, came up with this: "From the day you're born, 'til you're ridin' the hearse, there ain't nothin' so bad that it couldn't be worse." Now mind, this was about 1972 or '73. Going on fifty years ago. And yet I remember what he said as if it were yesterday.

OH, YEAH? WHAT DID SLIM KNOW ABOUT 2020?

Now, I don't know exactly when Slim Manley died. But I do know this: there's no way he's still alive. There's no way he hasn't taken that ride in the hearse. When I knew him, he must have been pushing sixty-five or seventy. And his leathery face looked every day of it. So when he laid that pearl of wisdom on me, he had no idea of what the year 2020 had in store for the us: COVID, the civil unrest that has swept our land from sea to shining sea, the wild fires that have scorched the western United States and even threatened the little burg of Grandby that Slim called home for so many years.

What would Slim say about 2020? Can it *really* get worse than this? You know the answer to that question: of course it can. But, at best, that's cold comfort. And if it does get worse, will that make us feel any better about 2020? I suppose. But only in the sense that it feels so good to quit hitting your head with a hammer.

A LONG AND WINDING ROAD

Which is a roundabout way of getting to what this blog's about: mental health, bipolar disorder, mania, and depression. And if there was ever a time when problems like these could bubble to the surface, this sure seems to be it. In fact, after heredity, stressful events are considered a leading cause of bipolar.

So what to do to keep the stress at bay? Here are some things that have been helpful to me: working out on a regular basis, getting enough sleep, limit time with the news—especially all the annoying political commercials. Stay in touch with family and friends—even if only by phone—and blog-ging, even if sometimes, like with this rascally, obstinate post, it only seems to make things worse.

And finally, and above all, keep this in mind during these trying times:

From the day you're born, 'til you're ridin' the hearse, there ain't nothin' so bad that it couldn't be worse.

2 4

FIGHT OR FLIGHT?

It wouldn't be too much of a stretcher to call my wife the Bird Lady. She loves 'em. We have bird feeders, bird baths, and hummingbird feeders all over the backyard. And they work. Freeloading birds of all kinds can't get enough of them.

Even though I don't know most of their names, there's an embarrassment of avian riches under the maple tree that spreads its branches over much of our backyard. Woodpeckers, both downeys and flickers. Goldfinch which, when the males are in their springtime finery, are like delightful yellow jewels darting through verdant shrubs that only a few weeks before were still shrouded in drab winter brown. Smug bluejays. And even the occasional sharp shinned hawk that comes screaming out of nowhere looking for a snack. And, sometimes, even getting a careless little bird that is then ripped apart at leisure. After which, only a mournful circle of feathers and a few tiny bones marks the spot of the kill on the back lawn.

THE STARS OF THE SHOW

As entertaining as the above cast of characters might be, they pale in comparison with our broad-tailed hummingbird friends. It's a toss-up as to whether they're best described as reckless or paranoid. One minute, the aggressor is furiously chasing a rival away from "his" feeder. The next, the tables are turned, and the aggressor is zigzagging into a neighbor's yard with the erstwhile "victim" hot on his broad tail.

The fact that there's a vacant feeder only a short distance on the other side of the yard apparently makes no difference; rather than a square meal, the fussing and feuding seems to be the real objective. It's hard to imagine how many precious calories these tiny creatures squander in their phony war games. But maybe it's not so hard to imagine—given that their bird brains can't be much larger than the tip of a well sharpened pencil.

These tiny birds, in short, provide graphic, living color demonstrations of what "fight or flight" looks like.

BIPOLAR DISORDER AND FIGHT OR FLIGHT

With the type of bipolar disorder that I've experienced, the fight phase comes in the form of mania. Restless energy. Self-confidence that can spill over to aggressiveness and a short temper. Delusions of grandeur. Financial recklessness. A racing mind that could go for days with little or no sleep. To one degree or another, I've known them all.

The flight phase? Depression. An "I can't bear to get out of bed this morning" kind of depression. A self-contempt that knew scarcely any bounds. A bleak darkness that left me yearning to escape myself. A darkness that left me carefully plotting my own demise.

And perhaps the most terrifying aspect of the experience? Knowing, with a virtual certainty, that the higher the high, the lower the low. Like seeing myself in a slow-motion car wreck. That went on for years. And then for decades.

HOW DO YOU SPELL RELIEF?

But I finally came to my senses and got help. For the last decade or so I've periodically met with a psychiatrist, and he's prescribed a bunch of pills I usually take at night before I lay me down to sleep. I suppose this list is a far cry from what else might be available out there, but it's what I know. And you'd best buckle up. These rascals are tongue twisting mouthfuls:

- Depakote: Goes by a host of names. Treats a range of illnesses, including bipolar, epilepsy, and migraines. No-one seems to know exactly why it works.
- Risperidone: In addition to bipolar, it takes on schizophrenia and the irritability associated with autism. Again, not entirely clear why it works.
- Metoprolol: I *think* I take it for the shakes. Which, I *think,* are a side effect of all the other drugs. But if it's not easy to keep track of all the pills, imagine how tough it is to remember what they're all supposed to do and the associated side effects.
- Zaleplon: A fast-acting sleeping med; adequate rest is important to help keep bipolar in check. It comes with all the usual precautions about addiction that accompany sleeping medications.

YOU PAYS YOUR MONEY AND YOU TAKES YOUR CHANCES

So, there you have it. One day in the life of the medicine cabinet of a guy with bipolar.

It's really kind of interesting to think about how they came up with the meds. The brightest minds in the business often don't seem to know why or how they work. So how *did* they come up with the right combinations of chemicals that did the trick? Did they line up a bunch of people like me who are bouncing off the ceiling one day and down in the dumps the next and then start having them swallow chemical cocktails until something seems to smooth things out—without turning them into zombies in the process? Or worse, killing them?

I honestly don't know. But I can say this for sure. This is one bird brain who's glad he's not still chasing my broad tail around the backyard.

25

TRILLIONS FOR WAR. NOT A CENT FOR MENTAL HEALTH. RELATIVELY SPEAKING

You up for a little history lesson? No? Too bad. It's my party and I'll cry if I want to.

Not long after the United States became the U.S., we got involved in an obscure and nearly forgotten naval conflict with France over money we owed to the French for their assistance in winning our Revolutionary War against Great Britain. This little fracas is known to history as the Quasi-War. Mercifully short and with few casualties, it largely ended because France, then under the iron hand of Napoleon, had much bigger fish to fry in the form of conquering Europe on land and trying to sink Britain at sea.

If there's one thing that's best remembered in this county about the war, it's probably the defiant declaration of Congressman Robert Harper: "Millions for defense, but not one cent for tribute." Harper was outraged because French diplomats had suggested that the dispute could be smoothed over, and war avoided with the payment of bribes. The dustup became known as the XYZ Affair. The Quasi-War broke out shortly thereafter.

THE MORE THINGS CHANGE, THE MORE THEY STAY THE SAME

Those digits 9/11 are indelibly etched in our minds by the September 11 terrorist attack that took down the World Trade Center, scorched the Pentagon, and caused nearly three thousand deaths and over twenty-five thousand injuries. But test yourself: what are the last two digits of that talismanic number?

If you're like me, it's been so many years that I have to google it to be sure. And yet, here we are, still at war in the Middle East. As of this writing we still have thousands of troops in Afghanistan and Iraq—although President Trump has mercifully ordered the withdrawal of many of them. Still, despite tens of thousands of U.S. casualties and trillions of dollars, we weren't able to win these "forever" wars.

Is it just me, or is it beginning to look like tribute might not be such a bad idea after all?

IT'S NOT JUST HOW THE MONEY'S BEEN SPENT. IT'S HOW IT WASN'T SPENT.

But while we're incinerating truckloads of Benjamins year after year on fruitless wars in the Middle East, we're largely ignoring our own people who are fighting their own very private wars with mental illness. In 2019 mental health spending in this country was about $225 billion. Certainly not an inconsequential amount. But given that much of this spending is paid for privately by individuals who can ill afford it, mental health needs in this country often go unmet.

This is especially so since 8% of the U.S. population, or 26 million people, don't have health insurance. Annual per capita spending on mental health in this country ranges from $37 in Florida to $375 in Maine. No, not huge sums. Unless, of course, you're out of a job with the COVID pandemic. And you're forced to choose between food and rent and getting the mental health counseling and anti-psychotic drugs that might, literally, spell the difference between life and death.

So, I have a simple proposal. How 'bout we bring our boys and girls home? And declare victory in a part of the world that, at least for the time being, seemingly has no interest in living peaceably with its neighbors? What makes us think that blowing up more stuff and killing more people is going to make peace magically break out?

How hard can it be to find better ways to use those trillions of dollars taking better care of people here at home?

26

DOUBLE TROUBLE

D o you remember what it felt like to wobble and weave down the sidewalk in a drunken stupor? I hope not.

But what if in addition to that boozy feeling, your mind, without warning and even when you're stone cold sober, occasionally goes on a tear that that leaves you irrationally high as a kite? Or in the depths of a suicidal despair?

Sound odd? It is. Take it from me. I've been to both places. And it's not because of too much alcohol—or some other kind of chemically induced state of altered consciousness. Instead, for me the drunken stagger is the result of a little understood but treatable tongue twister of a medical condition called normal pressure hydrocephalus, or the friendlier abbreviation NPH.

OK. But what's up with the wild swings between euphoria and the "been down so long it looks like up" depression? Again, it's a treatable psychiatric condition called bipolar disorder.

The thing that ties both ailments together is that they both afflict my brain. But, other than that, what's there to worry about?

ADDING INSULT TO INJURY

Ok. One brain screwup I can understand. But two? You gotta be kiddin! Nope: bipolar disorder in all it's crazy glory also.

But, again, I've been blessed. I've found a cure. Even if it took decades for me to face the music and get help. While the periodic trips to the shrink's office and the meds aren't perfect (think side effects), it's a whole lot better than nothing.

Again, the causes of bipolar disorder are poorly understood. But the most likely culprit is genetic inheritance.

Simply put, the disorder is characterized by mood swings between mania and depression that go far beyond normal happiness and sadness. The mania can produce a variety of reckless behaviors. Like the unnamed guy my psychiatrist told me about who went running down the hallway of the hospital screaming and naked.

Happily, I never got that bad. But sleeplessness? Irritability? The urge to spend recklessly? Delusions of grandeur? Involuntarily committed to a psychiatric hospital? Yep. Yep. And yep.

And on the downside: depression. Over twenty years, 6% of those with bipolar commit suicide; 30-40% engage in self-harm. It was only by God's grace that I didn't do myself in. In fact, I shudder to think how many times I carefully plotted my own demise. And me with a wonderful wife and three kids of whom I'm very proud.

But is there an upside of bipolar? Perhaps. There's considerable evidence that it's often paired with creativity. Here's a list of eight well known creative types who've had it:

- Russell Brand
- Catherine Zeta-Jones
- Kurt Cobain
- Graham Greene
- Nina Simone

- Winston Churchill
- Demi Lovato
- Alvin Ailey

"Only" one committed suicide.

BUT WHAT ABOUT THE TWOFER?

So, like me, you might be asking yourself, "What happens if you're bipolar *and* have NPH?

Good question. I don't have a clue. I snooped around a bit on the internet to try to find an answer, but nothing much popped up. And what little that did was in obscure medical journals that were *way* above my pay grade.

But I promise. Next time I go to see my shrink or the doctor I'll try to remember to ask about it. Unless, of course, it slips my mind and I get side-tracked by dementia, depression, or mania.

27

INTIMATIONS OF DEMENTIA?

The first thing that crossed my mind this fall when I'd forgotten both my wife's birthday *and* our anniversary, after I'd identified the nearest hidey-hole in which to duck and cover, was to come up with an excuse. And if there's a silver lining in the dark cloud of COVID that's hung over our heads going on forever, it's how handy it is when you need an excuse.

"Babe," I began, "you know how all these days are when we can scarcely get out of the house. They just run together. Heavens, I can scarcely keep track of what day of the week it is without looking at my phone. I'm very sorry. How can I make it up to you?"

And I'm not pulling that one out of thin air. It's just not the same "commuting" from our bedroom down the hall for another early Wednesday morning men's Bible study on—*ugh!* —Zoom. Rather than driving to church where there's hot coffee and doughnuts (even if they're the nasty King Soopers brand). And a room full of flesh-and-blood guys with their good-natured chatter. And their real, sometimes messy lives. After a while, all these house-bound, virtual days have the consistency of Jell-O pudding that's been run through a Blend-O-Matic.

"YOU NEED TO WRITE THINGS DOWN!"

But even COVID eventually wears thin as an excuse. In fact, the tread on that one's so far gone that it's virtually bald. So, I'm hearing the above quite a bit from the wife, Marleen. Or this variation: "Have you put Lucy's Christmas pageant on your calendar? Remember, I'm going to meet you at Mount Olive; I'm not going to be around to make sure you get you going. And give yourself plenty of time to get there." Annoying? Sure, but lamentably necessary.

Memory's a funny thing. Especially as you get older. Like Swiss cheese? "A firm, pale-yellow cheese having many holes." Put aside the color and that pretty much sums it up.

A TWOFER

But what's normal for a guy who rounds the bend on age seventy in a matter of weeks? And, especially for a guy who's gray matter is afflicted with both bipolar disorder *and* normal pressure hydrocephalous? Not really sure. But it can't be good.

Like just today. I was talking to Marleen about something or other as we sat at the kitchen counter eating lunch and watching our number-one ranked Gonzaga Bulldogs—GO ZAGS!—beat the Iowa State Hawkeyes in roundball. But, veering wildly off topic, for some reason she mentioned that she'd seen a fleeting image of what she thought was the Sweet Shop in a car commercial. "The Sweet Shop?" I replied. "It couldn't be. They've gone out of business. I drove by it not too long ago. All you could see through the windows was a bunch of junk."

But that got me thinking: *"How in the world was it that I'd driven by The Sweet Shop?* Yeah, I can remember the magnificent, solo road trip I'd taken a year ago—*or was it two?*—to visit cousins up in Oregon and Idaho. And, true, I'd been on the west side of Berthoud Pass for that. *But that couldn't be it.* Because on that trip I'd rented a car, crossed the Continental Divide on Trail Ridge Road and spent a night in Grand Lake before turning west on US 40 at Granby enroute to Jackson Hole, Yellow Stone, and Pendleton. Before looping back through Boise where I'd flown back to Denver. *I was miles away from going through Empire. How in the world had I seen the poor old Sweet Shop?"*

A FIGMENT OF MY IMAGINATION?

It was only after considerable mental gymnastics that I realized that, no, I wasn't hallucinating. And that, indeed, I'd gone over Berthoud Pass, driven through the tiny burg of Empire, and had actually seen the rundown old hulk of a building that used to house the Sweet Shop. It was when the kids had rented a house outside Grand Lake this last summer for their vacation. I'd driven up from Denver for a quick day visit with the gang, including Byron who'd come in from Omaha.

I heaved a sigh of relief: the wolves of dementia were still at bay. But I was distressed to think that the Sweet Shop was no more for this world. When I was in high school, it was a much-anticipated highlight after a day of skiing at Winter Park to pull over in Empire for one of their banana milk shakes. They were so thick and loaded with chunks of banana that it was impossible to drink them through a straw; you had to use a spoon.

So, just for old time's sake, I googled "sweet shop"; you never know what might pop up on the internet. And what to my wondering eyes appeared? The "Lewis Sweet Shop" website! But how'd I miss the store? I *know* that I'd seen junk piled to the rafters rather than the taffy pulling machine that used to tempt passing motorists through the big picture window out front.

WHO YA' GONNA CALL? THE SWEET SHOP!

And that's what I did. It was even a Denver area code. What'd I have to lose? The lady who answered was as nice as pie and visited with me like she had all the time in the world. "Yes," she said, "we moved out of the old location because the rent was too high, and the landlord wouldn't give us a break. So we are across the street now." Oh! The old switcheroo. No wonder I'd missed the new store:

"Made you look, you dirty crook. You stole your mother's
pocketbook.
Took a dime and bought some wine, and now you look like
Frankenstein!"

"We're the third family that's owned the store," she continued. "It's been in business since 1948." That's three years before this old man was even born. So, I guess it's not quite time to pack in the old brain. And who knows? Maybe next year I'll actually be able to remember Marleen's birthday. And our anniversary. But I'm not betting the farm on it.

IN THE DESTRUCTIVE ELEMENT
IMMERSE

The longer I live, the more apparent it is to me that my memory is a very queer thing. In fact, it's curiouser and curiouser. Ask me what I did yesterday, and you're likely to get a blank stare. Or, perhaps, "Uh, lemme think . . ." Yes, I'll probably come up with something eventually. But it's no cinch. It's why my family is insisting that I get a SLUMS test as I stare down my seventieth birthday in less than two weeks' time. So, yep, I'm going slumming next week at Kaiser.

As I was noodling in preparation to write this post, a mere fragment of a phrase from Joseph Conrad's novel, *Lord Jim*, came to mind. It's been about fifty years since I read that book. Literally. And, even though it's rated among the best one hundred English language novels of the twentieth century, it's far from an easy read. (I started listening to it again but quit after seven or eight chapters; it's tough sledding. Would it have been better had I been *actually* reading it? Can't say for sure, but probably.) But with only two or three stabs on Google with word combinations like, "destructive element immersion" or "joseph conrad destructive element" I found the phrase you see at the top of this post. And that's the entire phrase: *five words. In a lengthy novel. After fifty years.* And they tell me I need to get my memory checked. Go figure.

THE SEA FARING LIFE. WITHOUT GOING TO SEA.

I read *Lord Jim* during my, "I must go down to the sea again, the lonely sea and the sky" period. Scarcely out of my teens and rarely venturing beyond the borders of landlocked Colorado, Conrad's novel was, no doubt, the literary apogee of that particular obsession for me. Otherwise, it was pulp fiction pot boilers about skullduggery aboard tramp steamers. And the long walk through our sleepy, upscale suburban neighborhood one drizzly night in my "sea going" pea coat with an upturned collar. Unless you count the time I hitch-hiked from Denver to Provincetown, Massachusetts, with a layover at the YMCA in New York City. For a wet-behind-the-ears, cow town kid like me, that big, old, rambling Y in the canyons of Manhattan was a spooky place.

While in New York, I somehow made my way to a trade school or union hall that trained sailors for the merchant marine. I stood outside for a long time—I think it had a gang plank—debating whether to go in and find out what it took to enroll. But I eventually turned around and did nothing. I've been plagued with the "I'd rather study something than actually do it" syndrome for much of my life.

THE DIVINE COMEDY

For going on two months now, I've been reading Dante Alighieri's epic poem, the *Divine Comedy*. And I'm only about halfway through the eight-hundred-odd page account of the poet's imagined journey through hell, purgatory, and, finally, his ascent to heaven.

Written in the early fourteenth century by the Italian poet, philosopher, and politician, the Florentine's masterpiece makes

Lord Jim look like a cake walk. But I've stuck with it; its cantos come in bite-sized nibbles of six or seven pages with footnotes. In its strange way, it's addictive.

Don't ask me how I originally got turned on to *Commedia;* I suppose it was because it's considered one of the Mount Everests of world literature, in the same exalted company as the Bible or Shakespeare. But like Dante himself, it didn't take me long to conclude that this arduous journey is best undertaken with the help of a guide. Dante had three: Virgil, who personifies reason; Beatrice, who represents faith and divine revelation, and Saint Bernard of Clairvaux, who symbolizes mysticism and devotion to Mary.

I, on the other hand, am muddling through with one guide: Rod Dreher and his book, *How Dante Can Save Your Life.* After all, you can only read so much. An interesting guy in his own right, Dreher grew up in the bayous of Louisiana. But, like a moth to the flame, he was eventually captured by the bright political lights of Washington, DC, where he works as the senior editor of *The American Conservative.* Until, that is, he was recaptured by the barely discernible twinkle of his Louisiana home town, Starhill, a suburb of the nearest "big" town, St. Francisville, population 1,765.

Alongside his geographic meanderings, Dreher was also on a spiritual pilgrimage. Grown cold to his family's old-time Methodist religion, he enthusiastically turned to Catholicism until the church's relentless pedophile scandals caused him, his wife, and young children to embrace Greek Orthodoxy, Christendom's most ancient branch.

THE PRAYER

One of the practices favored by Greek Orthodoxy is The Jesus Prayer: "Lord Jesus Christ, Son of God, have mercy on me a sinner." Like the Catholic rosary, it's repeated over and over. Also like the rosary, a knotted chord is used to keep track of the number of times the prayer is uttered. When Dreher returned to his hometown, he fantasized that he would experience a warm embrace from his family and the small town where he'd grown up. He wrote about it in, The Little Way of Ruthie Lemming: A Southern Girl, a Small Town, and the Secret of a Good Life.

The reality was very different. His sister, Ruthie, had just lost her struggle with cancer, leaving behind a husband and three little kids. The grieving husband wanted very little to do with the Johnny-come-lately interloper from the big city. Dreher's father was on the downhill side of life and couldn't accept that his son had apparently forsaken his family, their faith, and the wide spot in the road that had given the Dreher clan meaning since the Civil War.

Dreher got so caught up in the undertow of all these family cross currents that his auto-immune system rebelled and he came down with the Epstein-Barr virus. He spent days—and then weeks—in bed with the curtains drawn; how his wife put up with him is a mystery to me. But one night, late, in bed next to his sleeping wife, there was a glimmer of hope.

After the fourth cycle around his daily prayer rope—three hundred prayers down and *only* two hundred more to go—a peace that passeth all understanding came over Dreher. Along with three words that he heard, not in his pointy head, but in his *heart*. The words threw him for a loop: *God loves me*. As he puts it, "It was the strangest thing, like someone was standing at my bedside, placing them into my chest.

Not *God loves you*, but *God loves me*. Just like that: *God loves me*.

THE *REST* OF THE STORY

How do the stories end? Not sure yet. I've *only* got about 450 more pages of Dante guiding me through the Byzantine political and ecclesiastical machinations of the early Italian Renaissance. Not to mention heaven, hell, and purgatory. And then there's Dreher wrestling with his own demons.

The peculiar hold of blood and soil in the Old South. A hold so tenacious that Dreher virtually abandoned his wife and family and took to his bed when he attempted to escape its gravitational pull.

And me? I'm holding on. But my memory's going. My seventieth is rapidly fading in the rearview mirror. I only answered ten of thirty questions today correctly. Next stop? The neurosurgeon.

29

MEMORY'S THE FIRST THING TO GO. WHAT WAS THE SECOND AGAIN?

W e had a family powwow over Christmas to discuss my memory. Along with other issues relating to my wife's and my advancing years. And believe you me, this getting old stuff isn't for sissies.

Our son, Byron, who works at Google, had driven home from Omaha; we don't get to see him face to face very often. Our two daughters live here in Denver with their families; they and their little ankle biters are frequent fliers at our house. Or at least they were before COVID.

The kids kicked things off by raising the possibility of our leaving our two-story house and moving into a ranch-style home. That didn't even get to the two-minute warning with my wife. In fact, Marleen sacked that idea with about ninety seconds to spare. And no timeouts allowed.

IN THE CROSSHAIRS

So, with leaving our home entirely off the table, all eyes turned my way. And, specifically, the way of my memory. Which was fine. I know that sometimes my memory's good, and sometimes it's terrible and not headed in the right direction. For example, a few days after our confab, I drove to Saint Joseph's Hospital to pick up our daughter Jocelyn. We're excited that she's expecting her third child. There was a little hiccup with her pregnancy that required minor surgery; everything turned out fine.

I don't know how familiar you are with the area around St Joe's, but in my opinion it's where directionally challenged old folks like me go to die, figuratively, of course. It's all one-way streets with no rhyme or reason. They dump you into expensive parking lots without warning. There are five- or even six-way intersections. So, did I turn up a bit late for my daughter's appointment? You betcha. But at least I eventually turned up. And like it or not, I'm going to give myself *some* credit for that achievement.

A CONTINUING CONVERSATION

Like my wife, our daughter Lauren is a nurse. What was her leadoff comment about my memory at the family meeting? "I think it should be a continuing conversation."

"I have no argument with that," I responded, "but the issue of my memory is a mystery to me. On the one hand," I went on, "I seem to have a good grasp of things that happened years ago, and sometimes even decades. Especially some of the things I've read. But ask me about what I did yesterday, and I'm often out to sea."

"Yes, Dad," offered Lauren, "long- and short-term memory can be very different. But it goes beyond just a matter of inconvenience or frustration. It can also be a safety issue. But there might be some medications that could help."

So, what do you do when you get a response like that? Of course: snoop around on the internet. And what do you get when you put "medications for memory loss" in the search bar? An answer, but nothing much I wanted to hear:

"The Food and Drug Administration has approved two

types of medications — cholinesterase inhibitors and meman-
tine — to treat the cognitive symptoms (memory loss, confusion, and problems with thinking and reasoning) of
Alzheimer's disease.

> As Alzheimer's progresses, brain cells die and connections
> among cells are lost, causing cognitive symptoms to worsen.
> While current medications cannot stop the damage
> Alzheimer's causes to brain cells, they may help lessen or
> stabilize symptoms for a limited time by affecting certain
> chemicals involved in carrying messages among the brain's
> nerve cells. Doctors sometimes prescribe both types of
> medications together." ("Medications for Memory, Cognition
> and Dementia-Related Behaviors," Alzheimer's Association)

So. There you have it. The Big A. The condition whose full
name, like Lord Voldemort's, must not be named.

TOO MUCH HOUSE

Next? Byron's turn. He reported that the last time all three kids
had been at the family condo in the mountains, our advancing
years had been the subject of a "late night, four-hour
discussion."

What did he touch on with us? Actually, more like what
didn't he mention? My memory. Our finances. The size of our
home. The daunting prospect of moving when our backs are
up against the wall, and we've run out of other choices. My
increasingly parlous physical and mental condition. The possibility of my stumbling and crashing down our home's two
flights of stairs sometime. Check. Check. And re-check.

"But in the end," he said, looking to first to his mother and
then to me, "it's what's important to you guys. Is it this house?
Or is it spending more time with your grandkids? Sure," he
said, "maybe you can do both. But it's no cinch."

SENSE AND SENSIBILITY

Our youngest, Jocelyn, is a sweetheart. Her husband, Aaron, brings home the bacon; she takes care of the kids. They live in a neighborhood that used to be working class, with boxy, fifties-style houses that used to be priced for working people whose families made them burst at the seams. But now the same modest fifties-era homes are saddled with the immodest prices that a city like Denver can command since it's been discovered and deemed "hot."

Jocelyn remained mute and listened for much of the discussion. But the dam finally broke. "It makes me so sad," she said, putting her face in her hands, the tears beginning to come, her shoulders heaving. "It's so hard to see you guys have to make decisions like these. So hard for us kids to see you getting older." I looked away. How could I be feeling pride? I immediately suppressed the smile that rippled over my face. Pride that this tender-hearted young woman felt my distress and mortality so deeply.

With Lady Macbeth, what else could I think of myself but, "Out, damned spot!"

WRITER'S BLOCK

As I was writing this post, I was beset by one of the worst cases of writer's block that I've ever had to contend with.

Day after day, I procrastinated. Could hardly even poke my head in Byron's old bedroom, now converted to my writing hidey hole, and endure the baleful stare of the blank computer monitor. Raid the refrigerator. Walk around the block. Hash it over with a pastor at church. TV. Anything but write.

And what, finally, worked? Don't ask me. If I knew, do you think I would have been stuck in what felt like an infinite loop as long as I was? Sort of like how I'd felt being lost in that maze of streets around St. Joe's hospital. But the more inter-

esting question is: why was it so bad this time? Isn't it obvious? How fired up would you be to write about your
deteriorating mental and, even, physical state? But what can I
cling to? This.

Reading a couple of chapters from *Charlotte's Web* to my
granddaughter Lucy this afternoon. The chapter about Wilbur
the pig wallowing in the manure. And Charlotte spelling
terrific in her web to save the pig from the slaughterhouse. I'll
cling to moments like that as long as God's tender mercies
permit.

30

IT'S NOT JUST PHYSICAL HEALTH.
IT'S ALSO MENTAL

Now, this is the kind of post that could get me in hot water for all kinds of reasons. Cold-hearted. Self-serving. You can probably come up with more reasons yourself without much trouble. My argument? That the COVID-19 pandemic has inflicted more harm because of the mental health fallout than the toll it has taken as a result of physical suffering and death.

"Yeah, *right*," I can just hear you saying, "over 500,000 deaths in the US alone. Over 2.6 *million* fatalities worldwide. And you're going to try to persuade me that the undoubted mental health suffering caused by COVID is *worse* than the millions who've lost their lives? You gotta be kidding! And," you can fairly add, "you're just navel-gazing since we all know by now that you're fixated on your own mental health problems with bipolar disorder and dementia."

Okay. I get that.

BUT CONSIDER . . .

Think for a moment about the emotional wreckage that this pandemic has left in its wake among *survivors*. The families that have been ripped apart by a loved one's untimely death. The depression. The economic stress endured by the countless folks who've lost their jobs. The entrepreneurs who've seen the business they've spent years building vanish beneath the COVID tidal wave.

According to an article in *Scientific American*, the population most severely impacted Are young adults. But the pandemic has by no means neglected adults. A recent study by the U.S. Centers for Disease Control and Prevention found up to four times as many adults suffering from anxiety and depression compared to 2019. Suicide? Drug abuse? The precise numbers, of course, vary. But the statistics are consistently worse post-COVID. And minority populations were almost invariably the most severely impacted.

STILL NOT CONVINCED?

Consider this. The rate of mental distress being seen now is worse than what was experienced after such large-scale traumas as September 11 and Hurricane Katrina. An unanticipated finding of the surveys was the outsized toll on young adults. In the CDC survey, 62.9 percent of eighteen to twenty-four-year-olds reported an anxiety or depressive disorder, a quarter said they were using more drugs and alcohol to cope with pandemic-related stress, and a quarter said they had "seriously considered suicide" in the previous thirty days.

Young adults were also the most affected age group in an unusual, real-time study that tracked the rapid rise in "acute distress" and depression at three points between mid-March and mid-April. But why is it surprising that young people seem to be more severely impacted by the pandemic?

It's not the young, in general, who are getting sick and dying. Why are they so upset? Consider the milestones and connections that many of them are missing. Their buddies at school. Graduation ceremonies. Weddings. Their senior year of high school and college. With raging hormones and social pressures, navigating young adulthood is tough under the best of circumstances. Pile on COVID clamp downs and these are far from the best of times for young people.

ROUND UP THE USUAL SUSPECTS

And what are a lot of folks doing when they're cooped up at home with too much time on their hands? You guessed it: TV. And the remedy? Watch less of it. Especially the news shows that take particular delight in feeding us a steady diet of doom and gloom. And that's not just me spouting off.

The same CDC study recommends that we "limit media consumption and avoid sensationalist reports." But it's not just about what we *shouldn't* do. In the same *Scientific American* article reference above, Psychologist James Pennebaker of the University of Texas advises that "maintaining social contacts—via Zoom, phone, or other COVID-safe methods—is also vital."

"YEAH, BUT WHAT ABOUT YOU?"

Good question. Between my bipolar disorder, NPH, and creeping dementia, I have more than my fair share of mental disorders to worry about. But the strange thing is that I seem to be doing pretty well in that department. Ten to twelve years back, bipolar pretty much had me on the ropes. I'd be down in a suicidal swamp one week and bouncing off the walls—and terrifying my family—when in the grips of a mania the next. But I eventually found a shrink who got me on the right meds and things have pretty well leveled off.

As an aside, getting adequate sleep is an important compo-nent of keeping the bipolar genie in the bottle. And, because I watched this podcast the other day, I went to the Calm website and signed up. The next two nights, when I woke up and couldn't go back to sleep, I set my phone on the nightstand, started listening, and poof! Like magic, I was out cold in about ten minutes. Don't ask me how. But I sure prefer admittedly sappy music and happy talk to sleeping pills.

As for the normal pressure hydrocephalous? Admittedly, not so great. They've checked the brain shunt that was put in my head repeatedly over the years. And it's functioning as it should. But the wet, wacky, and wobbly symptoms seem to continue to get worse—albeit slowly—as I age. I suppose that's why they say this getting old stuff isn't for sissies!

HOLD THE PRESSES!

My wife and I went in to see my new Kaiser GP yesterday to discuss my creeping dementia. Using their nifty online communication tool, he got back to me today. But that's the topic for my next post.

31

IT'S OFFICIAL! THE CURSE OF THE LIVING DEAD

onepezil. Now, how would you pronounce that? "done-PEZIL?" WRONG! The fact sheet that came with the little bottle of innocuous looking pills that I picked up the other day says it's (doh-NEP-eh-zil). OK. But, how bad can that be? Well, not that bad, I guess. Until you read the first couple lines of the fact sheet: "Donepezil is used to treat confusion (dementia) related to Alzheimer's disease. It does not cure Alzheimer's disease, but it *may* improve memory, awareness, and the ability to function. This medication is an enzyme blocker that works by restoring the balance of natural substances (neurotransmitters) in the brain."

The emphasis, by the way, is mine. And, who knows, it might work long enough so that I can describe how this process begins to unfold. Before I become a . . . what? A drooling insentient slumped in a chair in the corner of some nursing home? Or, the homey euphemism favored by the industry that caters to those with dementia: a "memory care neighborhood"?

OH. DID I MENTION THE SIDE EFFECTS?

Of course, not. I forgot. But I just remembered to check out that part of the fact sheet: "Nausea, vomiting, diarrhea, loss of appetite/weight loss, dizziness, drowsiness, weakness, trouble sleeping, shakiness (tremor), or muscle cramps may occur as your body adjusts to the drug." Additional possible side effects? Nightmares. Yeah, I think I can relate to that during the last few nights. At least if my memory isn't playing tricks on me. (You, I presume, know how crazy dreams can be.)

But the good news? "These effects usually last one to three weeks and then lessen." And the *really* good news? So far, so good—at least as far as I can tell. But I'll be on the lookout. And keep you posted if things change.

A bit of snooping on the internet turned up additional information. "Donepezil appears to result in a *small* benefit in mental function and ability to function. Use, however, has *not* been shown to change the progression of the disease." And then this: "Treatment should be stopped if no benefit is seen."

SO, WHERE'S THAT LEAVE ME? BESIDES A RUMBLING GUT.

In a word: *curious.* That's why I just set an appointment with the doctor to go over Donepzil's "small benefits" and how, if at all, the drug might actually help. But what can I say? I suppose this, ripped from a dementia website I stumbled upon from merry old England (where dementia has become the leading cause of death):

> Progressive brain cell death will eventually cause the digestive system, lungs, and heart to fail, meaning that dementia is a terminal condition. Studies suggest that, on average, someone will live around ten years following a dementia diagnosis. However, this can vary significantly

between individuals, some people living for more than twenty years, so it's important to try not to focus on the figures and to make the very most of the time left. (What's the life expectancy for someone with dementia? MyHomeTouch.com)

And finally? This. The Grim Reaper is going to get me. One way or another. And the real question is whether I'm ready to meet my Maker. And the answer? Certainly not! At least not on my own merits. But on the merits of Christ? Absolutely! What other choice do I have?

FIRST IMPRESSIONS CAN BE DECEPTIVE

The first thing I saw as I walked through the door of the Littleton Clinic? Pills. Row on row of bottles of what I knew were inevitably going to be vitamins and supplements. They were neatly arranged on shelves beneath the chest high window on the far side of the waiting room.

"Great," I thought, "a snake oil salesman." Or, more precisely, a snake oil sales*woman*. "Just what I need. More pills."

I'd gotten an early start for the 9:45 appointment. Between the snowstorm that was predicted for that morning, which would have hopelessly snarled traffic during rush hour on the miles-long drive (us retired folk don't *commute*), I didn't want to be late. But I caught a break; I beat the storm and traffic was light. The only fly in the ointment? I nearly changed lanes right into a small car just before making the right turn into the clinic parking lot. A wreck would've *really* done me in.

THE LAME AND THE HALT

"I have a 9:45 appointment," I said to the receptionist as she looked up from behind the half wall that separated her from the small lobby. "I'm Spencer Swalm. I think I filled out all my new patient forms online. I'm early."

"That's fine," she smiled, "have a seat. Dr. Hopp will be with you soon."

"Well," I said to myself with a skeptical look around the busy waiting room, "we'll see about that."

I found a chair next to the shelves of vitamins, minerals, and supplements. Bottles of them were perched over my left shoulder, rank on rank, three and four deep. I took my copy of *The End of Alzheimer's Program* out of my lap and propped it up against the leg of my chair. I'd given up reading it; way above my pay grade. But it wasn't long before an elderly woman saw the title, stepped up, and asked from behind her mask, "I've heard about that book. What do you think about it?"

"Well," I said, "it's pretty complicated. But you can take a look at it if you'd like."

"Thanks," she replied, "but probably not. That's not why we're here." With that, she tottered back to her husband's side, whose slicked over gray hair looked like it was falling out in clumps. The woman and her husband looked like they pretty much fit right in with most of the rest of the patients in the room.

I couldn't help wondering, "Do I?" I hoped not. To my surprise, I didn't have much longer to wait. The receptionist craned up her head, peered over the half wall, and said, "Mr. Swalm? This way," gesturing toward the door that led to the back. A man and a woman met me; turned out that the man shadowing the intake nurse was new. Taking me to an exam room, they went through the usual routine: height, weight, a few questions.

"We see that you filled out the online new patient question-naire; we appreciate that. Do you have anything to add?"

"No," I replied, "except my wife didn't get the chance to fill out the form asking about how she thinks my Alzheimer's is progressing. She's got her hands full with some conditions of her own."

"That's not a problem," the nurse replied. "If we need it, we can always get it later. Dr. Hopp will be with you shortly." And the two of them left.

THE DOCTOR AND HER SCRIBE

Maria Hopp, M.D., soon walked in followed by yet another assistant. The assistant sat down at a small desk in the corner of the exam room and opened her laptop. As I recall, the assistant never opened her mouth; instead, she was constantly typing, like a court reporter.

On my lap sat my copy of *The End of Alzheimer's*. Dr. Hopp describes herself online as being a "certified practitioner" of the protocol described in the book. Dr. Hopp sat slightly to my left. Above what might have been a homemade mask, there were dark circles beneath her bright, alert eyes.

"Well, Mr. Swalm," she began, "tell me what's going on."

"Well," I started, not very originally, "it's complicated. My family thinks my memory is failing. My Kaiser doctor has prescribed Donepezil to treat Alzheimer's. One of your patients is a ninety-year-old friend of a friend at church. I understand he's seeing you for Alzheimer's."

Dr. Hopp nodded, indicating that she was familiar with the patient.

"Anyway, the friend who saw the post I wrote about being prescribed Donepezil suggested I give you a call. I looked at your website and saw that you follow the Bredesen protocol," gesturing towards the book. "So, I got it, called, and set this appointment."

"Okay," she responded, "but that's not the end of it, is it? I've seen the online forms you gave us. You also have normal pressure hydrocephalus."

"Yes," I replied, "and that's where it gets complicated. You can see," I said, twisting my head and showing her the back, "that I've got a brain shunt for the NPH. The outline of the tube shows because I got a haircut the other day. And," I went on, "even *that's* not the end of my brain problems. I'm also bipolar, for which I take a couple of medications every day. So, like I said, it's complicated. How do you unpick it all?"

YOU ARE WHAT YOU EAT

"I've started reading the book," I continued, "but, as you know, for a layperson like me, it's complex."

She nodded.

"However, I've begun making some changes in my diet based on what I read. I've cut out a lot of the carbs, bread, and cereal. I've already seen my weight go down some. Trying to eat more veggies, which isn't too tough since my wife is supportive of that for both our sakes. But I've struggled with breakfast since giving up cereal. I eat more eggs, but I also wonder about that."

With that, the doctor rushed out the door and came back bearing a small plastic bowl and a handout. "Here, this might be a good breakfast option," she said, allowing me to peer into the bowl's contents and giving me the recipe for Dr. Hopp's Breakfast Porridge.

To be honest, the brief glimpse into the bowl left me with the impression of a couple of raspberries floating on a puddle of used engine oil. But I've since enjoyed her breakfast concoction of chia, hemp, flax seeds, and cinnamon, stirred into almond milk and almond butter, all topped with a couple of berries. Although I've never tried SAE 30, I'm confident Dr. Hopp's porridge doesn't taste a bit like used motor oil.

ENOUGH, ALREADY!

By now, you've probably had more than your fill of this post. I know I have. And is the Bredesen Protocol going to ward off my Alzheimer's? Don't ask me; I'm clueless. Although the book's cutesy chapter titles are, at best, annoying and off-putting, and, at worst, nearly useless in finding what you're looking for, its basic tenets of a largely plant-based, organic diet, exercise, adequate sleep, stress reduction, mental stimulation, and good oral health make sense under almost any circumstance. Does the implementation of the protocol require a significant commitment? Definitely: "coaching" for thirty minutes a week for six months. And several thousand dollars. But "significant" compared to what?

I have five young grandkids. And another on the way this August. Compared to being sufficiently sentient to see at least some of those kids graduate from high school? College? Maybe even get married? No, for my time and money, to be granted the blessing to be around to witness and enjoy even a fraction of those landmark events would be a bargain.

SURVIVING THE CRAZY TWINS

O K. Let's keep this simple. How do you survive when you have *two* disorders that afflict your brain? Both of which can drive you crazy. And one of which *has already* resulted in your being involuntarily committed to a psychiatric hospital for a two-week "visit"? And the other of which might, in the not-too-distant future, see me wind up slumped and drooling in the corner of the memory care unit of a nursing home? In a couple of words? *Very carefully*.

YOU DO WHAT YOU CAN

I've heard of Bon Jovi. But I don't think I've ever heard one of his songs—I'm a classical music kind of guy. Press me, and I would have said he's a limey—part of the British Invasion of yore. Why? Can't tell you. Turns out, however, he's a rocker from Jersey, right here in the good ole US of A.

In any event, he and his band cut a COVID, song / video recently called "Do What You Can." What, you might fairly ask, does that have to do with the crazy twins? Probably not a whole lot. Except the phrase is what first came to mind for this post as I've wrestled with describing how I've tried to first identify and then get help solving the two-fold wackiness of my brain. Which, as you probably know, is an organ that has been described as the most complex object in the universe. (With, no doubt, the exception of the ineffable, yet personal Lord God Himself.)

UP AND DOWN. DOWN AND UP.

That's pretty much how the oldest of my two brain buddies works. I was first seized with a doozie of a bout of depression when I broke up (for around the umpteenth time) with my first serious girlfriend around the age of twenty-two. (Be sure to mention to my wife of forty years—when you see her—that she was also the last serious girlfriend I had before we tied the knot.) So bad a case of the blues, in fact, that it drove this pagan, for the first time in years, through the doors of a church I wondered by in the People's Republic of Boulder. About an hour later, I emerged as a perma-dyed-in-the-wool Christian. And then, within a few days, I took off on my first wild bout of mania, during which—get this—I briefly fantasized that I was the second coming of Jesus Christ. *Please!* Don't tell anyone about that.

Oh, did I mention that I was seized with that first bout of mania while I was on a pheasant hunting trip with Dad and one of his buddies in northeast Colorado? You know, we went out to shoot guns all over the place. Can't get into the gory details here, but I thought Dad was acting weird about my newfound faith. My angry, no doubt paranoid accusations about what Dad had in mind for his nice Browning over and under late on a dark night when we were cooped up in an old motel somewhere near the little town of Sterling meant no one got much sleep.

No wonder a couple of Denver sheriffs showed up at the folks' house when we got home, nearly frog-walked me to their patrol car, locked me in the back seat behind a black metal grill, and took me to the Mount Airy Psychiatric Hospital. Where, just like Hotel California, you can check-in, but you can never leave—at least without a court order.

SO, WHAT WAS WORSE?

The depression. No question. Heck, maybe I couldn't sleep much when I was manic. And I occasionally scared the bejeebers out of my wife and family with my high jinks. But blow my brains out? No. The exact opposite: happy dancing. I've written about the *bi* in bipolar before.

But the worst of the worst for depression? Amway. At least five years of beating our heads against that impenetrable wall. Rejection after rejection after rejection. Exhausting, sleepless drives from one coast to the other for quarterly weekend "major" functions like Free Enterprise and Dream Weekend. Jump in the car after work on Thursday, drive all night to places like Louisville or Sacramento or Orlando.

Join a crowd of thousands of fellow distributors doing the wave. And hear speaker after speaker say the same thing: "You can get rich too, just like us!" Then, in the wee hours of the night, stagger upstairs to our bedroom, collapse on the bed, sleep a few hours, and then do it all over again. Sure, a few did get rich. About as many as you could count on your fingers and toes in that huge crowd.

AND IF THAT WEREN'T ENOUGH

Normal pressure hydrocephalous, or more mercifully NPH. Of course, I've written about this one before. It has three symptoms: lousy balance, urinary incontinence (like the time I got stuck in traffic and pulled into the garage with sopping pants and a bucket seat full of piss—but you don't have to tell anyone about that little *oops!*) and as if that weren't enough, dementia and eventually Alzheimer's. Like, sitting in the corner of the memory care unit of the nursing home and wondering "Who *are* these people?" when your wife, kids, and grandkids drop by for a visit.

So, there you have it. The crazy twins. But never forget what my old ditch-digging boss, Slim Manley, used to say:

"From the day you're born 'till you're ridin' the hearse, there ain't nothin' so bad that it couldn't be worse."

THE BIG REVEAL!

N ow, understand. I've never been very well disciplined about keeping my nose to the grindstone. And perhaps even more to the point, "The best-laid plans of plans of mice and men often go awry." (The Scot bard Rabbie Burns's original of that hackneyed phrase is infinitely more lilting, but nearly as incomprehensible to us moderns: "The best laid schemes o' mice an' men / Gang aft a-gley.") Me included: "Gang aft a-gley." *Whaaaat?* But that's beside the point.

The *real* point is that this blog I've been chipping away at for yea so many years actually *does* have a bigger goal in mind. And here's the general idea of what I'm thinking going forward. Assuming, of course, I can keep my nose to the grindstone. And that my best-laid schemes don't *gang a-gley.*

Drum roll . . . *wait for it . . .* **the publication of a memoir!** Titled? You guessed it: **Surviving the Crazy Twins** And if anyone out there is asking themselves, "I wonder where *that* came from?" We know exactly who to blame: *me.* 'Cause if you haven't caught the general drift of my life by now, my communication skills are so lost in the throes of a bipolar break that you should probably call the guys in the little white coats. Tell them to put me in a straitjacket and have them hustle me straight down to Pueblo. Or, you should give my family a shout and let them know that the old man is so badly addled by the incipient Alzheimer's brought on by my old companion, NPH, that they better get him checked into a memory care unit of the nearest nursing home. *Pronto.*

But let's assume, for the sake of argument, that things aren't that bad, and you *do* get the drift of what I've been beavering away at over the last few years in this blog. Now, if this "scheme" comes out of the blue to you, I think I can understand. And I certainly won't hold it against you. Heck, even as I was writing this post, I reviewed some of the material I've posted about my experiences with bipolar and Alzheimer's and thought, "How in the world did that long, rambling thing contribute to where I'd like this to end up?"

A MATTER OF PERSPECTIVE?

I can only hope that I'm just too close to this thing. My life. This blog. These posts that I've read and reread and poked and prodded so many times. So close to it all that I sometimes fear that I've lost the forest for the trees. But come what may, I'm determined to soldier on.

True, there's a few more posts to go, maybe even as few as one or two, before I'll be ready to start wrapping things up for the memoir. And, no doubt, some extraneous events in my life will pop up to distract me from keeping the main thing the main thing. But that's okay. My life is like most of yours: it's never proceeded in a nice, linear fashion. And this blog's pretty much the same. But, on the other hand, as I'm rounding the turn into the home stretch for age seventy-one, no-one lives forever. Including me.

If I ever want this memoir to see the light of day, I'd better keep my nose to the grindstone. And hope, and pray, that my best laid plans don't *gang aft a-gley.*

35

PILL POWER?

By now, you know that I've been diagnosed with Alzheimer's disease. And, in fact, I've been prescribed the medication donepezil to treat it. Which, unfortunately, "appears to result in a small benefit in mental function and ability to function." That's the bad news.

THE GOOD NEWS

The good news is that there's a brand new drug on the market: Aduhelm or aducanumab. How in the world do they come up with these goofy names?! It has received preliminary FDA approval for treatment of the illness. The advantage of Adulelm? "It's the first therapy," according to the FDA, "to target and affect the underlying disease process rather than just the symptoms." A possible downside? The drug can cause swelling of the brain, which, although probably temporary, is of particular concern for me because I already have a fat head. Or, actually, a swollen brain with NPH.

There is a definite downside to Aduhelm, the exorbitant cost. One year of Aduhelm will set you (or Medicare) back a cool $56,000. It's provoked a firestorm of controversy. Bottom line? My doc tells me I'm not a good candidate for the new Alzheimer's wonder drug because I already have a swollen head, er, brain.

SO, WHAT'S A GUY WITH A FAT HEAD TO DO?

You guessed it. More pills. Granted, many of the pills that Dr. Maria Hopp recommends follow the Bredersen anti-Alzheimer's protocol and seem pretty garden variety. But taken together, all the vitamins and supplements that I'm popping morning and night barely fit into a *large* seven-day pill organizer, which immediately suggests a question: how in the world did I ever get so old?!! Simple: one day at a time.

But ready or not, here's a rundown on all the pills my favorite pusher, Dr. Hopp, who, for all the world, appears to be an intelligent physician with a gentle sense of humor—and, moreover, seems to be a straight shooter—has me on:

- *Multivitamin:* Nothing new here; been taking these forever.
- *CoQ10:* I dare you to figure this one out. In fact, unless you're a real pill geek, I dee-double dare you. According to WebMD, this supplement is an anti-oxidant that protects cells from damage and is available in many foods. For my purposes, preliminary research suggests that it may help ward off Alzheimer's. Aha!
- *Vitamin D:* The Sunshine Vitamin is generally recognized as conducive to good bone strength. Something important to me, a guy who's had more sports related fractures than I care to recall. Or that you want to hear about. But it's also worth noting that the Mayo Clinic reports that "low levels of vitamin D in the blood are associated with cognitive decline." So, what's a guy have to lose for upping

the sunshine factor when he's already been branded with the scarlet A?

- *Probiotics:* The little "bugs" found in fermented foods like yogurt and sauerkraut. To my surprise, there's actually some research suggesting that these rascally microbes may help us old codgers battling Alzheimer's.
- *DHA Omega:* Basically, fish oil. I've actually been taking it for years at the recommendation of my psychiatrist to ward off the acute misery and wild euphoria of bipolar disorder. Research now suggests it might also be helpful in warding off dementia. So, lucky me. *A twofer!*
- *Vitamin E:* Found in many foods besides vegetable oil, this versatile vitamin (and that, folks, is an alliteration) is required for the proper functions of many of our organs. "Fine," you say, "but what's it got to do with Alzheimer's?" This: "it doesn't seem to prevent Alzheimer's disease from developing. But in people who already have Alzheimer's disease, taking vitamin E along with some anti-Alzheimer's medicines might slow down memory loss."
- *Curcumin:* Best known to us non-nerd types as turmeric, this is the bright yellow spice of Asian cuisine. While its efficacy for treating dementia is controversial, an article on the National Institutes of Health website suggests that the compound may be useful in delaying the onset of the disease. My take? You pays your money and you takes your chances.
- *Pregnenolone:* I'm no internet search wizard, but I couldn't find anything suggesting it helps with Alzheimer's. Guess I'll have to ask Dr. Hopp.
- *Vitamin A:* Again, generally a good idea. But helpful with Alzheimer's? I couldn't find it.
- *Zinc: The Journal of Neuroscience* reports that "zinc

supplementation was associated with reduced risk and slower cognitive decline, in people with Alzheimer's disease and mild cognitive impairment." Chalk one up for the good guys.

- *Copper:* Great. Some reputable sources say it hurts. Others say it helps. Answer? I guess you picks your poison.
- *Ashwagandha:* An herbal remedy for stress commonly used in Asia and Africa, it's a head scratcher for me when it comes to Alzheimer's.
- *Testosterone:* Given my history of bipolar disorder, this one really makes my wife nervous. But what's she think? That her seventy-year-old husband is going to morph into a muscle-bound sex maniac? Whatever. But research suggests that low testosterone levels in older men with memory problems may signal progression to Alzheimer's disease. And trust me. My wife *definitely* thinks I have memory problems. But, for the sake of domestic harmony, I promise to ask my shrink her opinion about this one.

THE FLY IN THE OINTMENT

So, there you have it. The laundry list of pills and potions that I take at the suggestion of Dr. Hopp. And I've probably missed some. But the real question is: Do they actually help? And before I go on, let me add, "I sure hope so!" All those pills don't come cheap. Of course, Drs. Hopp and Bredersen believe so. But what about third parties?

Now, I'm certainly no expert. And I can't claim to have thoroughly researched the question. But a look at the internet suggests skepticism.

The Lancet is a weekly peer-reviewed general medical journal. Highly regarded, it is among the world's oldest and best-known general medical journals. And what does *The Lancet* have to say about the end of Alzheimer's? Exercise extreme caution. In an extensively footnoted article in the May 2020 edition, numerous red flags were highlighted, including undisclosed conflicts of financial interest, shoddy research techniques, and an unbalanced presentation of proposed scientific findings.

Want more? Actually, *much* more? A lengthy research paper by the Global Council on Brain Health, a worldwide consortium of scientists and health professionals working in the areas of human cognition, concluded about the efficacy of supplements for treating a disorder like Alzheimer's that, to put it mildly, it's not encouraging. So, will I continue? I certainly intend to have a heart to heart with Dr. Hopp. Stay tuned.

THIS RUINOUS WRITING LIFE

WRITE THE BOOK. SWEAT THE SNUBS LATER.

When I retired a few years back, I decided to get serious about this writing thing. Boy, talk about serious. Seriously messed up. Started with a blog. Figured I'd dip my toe in the shallow end. So I hired someone to help me set it up. And, as far as I know, she did a fine job. That done, I started pecking away at a nearby library.

"The library?" you ask. "Why not at home? You're retired; don't you have a spare bedroom?"

"Sure," I reply. "But there are a couple of very good reasons for the library. No TV. And no refrigerator. Can you think of two better reasons than that?"

THE FIELD OF DREAMS

I soon learned that just because you build it, that doesn't mean they'll come. I've posted dozens and dozens of times over the past several years. And can probably count my followers on one hand. If I'm lucky, two.

True, the blog's political take was probably off-putting to

many for the first few years. But who wouldn't want to learn about my Crazy Twins? Bipolar disorder and incipient dementia—or Alzheimer's. Sure, most people aren't afflicted with them *personally*. But the internet's a big place. There's a lot more than "many" out there.

It's estimated that 50 million people have Alzheimer's worldwide, over 6 million in the U.S. alone. The financial burden in the U.S. is over *$200 billion per year.* For every person suffering from the disease in this country, nearly two people serve as caregivers, or 11 million. At some point, even I can take a hint.

So, time to give up? Hardly. No, it was time to raise my sights. And rather than spending nickels and dimes to have someone help me with the technical aspects of blogging that mystified me, it was time to start spending some serious coin.

BARGAIN BASEMENT

For a while, I joined something called hope*writers. Its approach is writing coaching for the masses. They maintain a large online library of writing resources. There are weekly video conferences. The appeal is almost exclusively to Christian women. (I didn't know that 'til after I'd joined.)

As a group they're best described as relentlessly upbeat and chirpy. There was an in-person meeting in the Denver area for those interested in memoir. I stuck with them until I went to the meeting. With tens of thousands of Facebook followers, I don't think they'll miss me.

NEEDLESS MARKUP

I'll be the first to admit that hope*writers is a bargain compared to the many "writing coaches" out there. I used to practice law—it's been a long time—but some of the hourly fees that these writing coaches charge might even make an attorney blush. And trust me, that's not easy to do. Then there're the "writers' retreats."

There's one called the Red House in California's Sierra Nevadas. There aspiring writers can get in touch with their inner muse for up to a cool $1,600 a week, rub shoulders with published writers/coaches, escape the TV and the refrigerator (but not gourmet meals), and slumber in "cozy" rooms that look like they'd fit right in at a Fairmont. Private coaching runs an additional one hundred and fifty bucks per hour. That not enough to scare you off? Try $4,250 for ten days with Memoir Tours in Ireland. Or Breakthrough Writing Retreats at a sweet-looking oceanside resort in Costa Rica for at least a cool $3,000.

If these writing retreats don't get your creative juices flowing, then the folks behind them will probably just have to round up another gang of aspiring, but terminally blocked, writers to cover their all-expense paid vacations to some other exotic location next year. Is it just me, or do you get the feeling that most of these writers don't make their living writing? Instead, they earn their keep by trying to teach other writers to get just good enough to start their own coaching gig.

You start looking at all the writers who show up at these retreats to teach, and you wonder how the *New York Times* has enough column inches to list all the number-one best-selling authors! Something tells me that, regardless of how many books I might someday sell (fingers crossed!), I won't be invited to teach at the Red House. Or Memoir Tours. Or Breakthrough Writing Retreats. Or the no doubt countless others that I had neither the time nor the patience to google. Oh, well. I better get the book written first. And worry about the snubs later.

TERMINAL?

N ow, there's an ominous word. As in, of course, cancer. Mercifully, that's not what afflicts me. Or, for an author (if I dare use that exalted term), something scarcely less terrifying: terminal writer's block. But that's not it either.

No, I think what has me by the throat might better be described as techno-terminal. In other words, this blankety-blank computer and all its barely comprehensible programs. Let me explain.

TWIN ONE

I'm wrestling with this memoir tentatively titled, *The Crazy Twins*.

In the first instance, it's about my experiences with bipolar disorder. How my first go-round with the condition led to my parents having me involuntarily committed to a psychiatric hospital as a young man. Following a hunting trip. You know. The whole works: shotguns, an angry confrontation with my dad, the cops hauling me away in a paddy wagon. And I'm not even a fan of Sigmund Freud and his Oedipus Complex.

Finally, with the support of my wife, a good shrink, and the right combination of psych meds, I finally emerged, years later, at the other end of this dark tunnel of wild rides up and life-threatening downs.

Oh, and how could I forget? With the help of this guy Jesus that I encountered in the midst of this craziness, who has sustained me through thick and thin ever since. And how long is that? Oh, about fifty years or so.

TWIN TWO

The second twin? Nearly as much "fun": dementia, a.k.a., Alzheimer's. But of much more recent vintage than the bipolar. This is one that sneaks up on you; it's sure taken me by surprise. In fact, the process is so gradual that if you pressed me, I might respond with, "Huh? What are you talking about? *Me* with Alzheimer's?"

"Actually, yes," I'd reply. "That's what the doctors tell me."

They've even prescribed pills, Donepezil, that I swallow every day. True, whether those pills actually *work* is a matter of some debate in the medical community. And, yes, there's a new wonder drug on the market that's supposed to be more effective: Aduhelm. But even this new drug has provoked a firestorm of controversy.

First, because it's outrageously expensive: a cool $56,000 per person per year. Given the tidal wave of Alzheimer's that's sweeping the nation, some believe this pill, all by its little-bitty self, could threaten the financial viability of Medicare. The second reason for all the *sturm und drang*? Because not even all the experts agree the medication actually *works*. But if your Medicare goes belly up, don't blame me. Why? Because I'm not a candidate for the new wonder drug.

One of its potential side effects is to cause the brain to swell. And I already have a fat head: Normal Pressure Hydro-cephalous. To relieve the pressure, they've installed a brain shunt (check out the link; medical technology is amazing). In fact, if you catch me within a few days of one of my el cheapo haircuts at Great Clips, you can actually see the shunt outlined in the close cropped hair at the back of my skull.

TECHNOPHOBIA

If The Crazy Twins aren't enough to put the fear of God in a person, what in the world can do the trick? Well, isn't it obvious? **Technology!** And before you dismiss me as hopelessly retrograde in terms of tech, consider all these word-processing programs I've used:

- **Pages:** When my memoir was little more than a gleam in its creator's eye, I started work in this MacBook word processing program. And while there was some text worthy of making it to the final draft (like the account of my stay at the funny farm), my early efforts to effectively use this app were laughable.
- **Storyworth:** From Pages, I moved on to something called Storyworth. It's a primitive word processing program intended to allow the sharing of stories within a small family circle. A Christmas gift from exactly which family member I no longer have a clue (this Alzheimer's is the *dickens*), it nonetheless houses some portions of the memoir worth preserving (like pulling all-nighters to drive to big Amway rallies all over the country—perhaps two of the *worst* things you can do for bipolar).
- **WordPress:** Probably the most widely used, versatile, and sophisticated blogging apps, WordPress hosts the vast majority of my posts.
- **Orbit:** Never heard of 'em? No wonder your marketing program isn't working. They're the ones who've taken my blog to the next level. Now, if they

can just help me tie this whole crazy contraption
together and get this darn (that's "d-a-r-n") memoir
over the finish line!

THE HOME STRETCH?

Now, I confess it's been a dreadfully long run. And to say that
I've been dilatory when it comes to keeping my nose to the
memoir writing grindstone is a gross understatement. But I'll
take what comfort I can from the fable of the tortoise and the
hare; victory doesn't always go to the swift. It goes, in some
cases, to the persistent. But even better? Swift *and* persistent.

Because I'm pushing seventy-one, and at least on this side
of eternity my allotted number of days certainly isn't growing,
and none of those I have left is guaranteed, if there is one thing
going for the Crazy Twins it might be *timing*. Which is well
illustrated by the many the folks around me today at the
library where I'm writing: virtually all of them are wearing
masks in response to the pandemic. Bizarre, stressful, unprece-
dented times. Times no-one predicted. So, who knows? Maybe,
just *maybe*, folks might be interested in the story of a guy
whose brain got sideswiped by life not just once but twice.
First, with bipolar disorder, a mental illness that can send it
wildly careening from irrational highs. To equally irrational
lows. And second, Alzheimer's. Which brings me to the
second thing that might give my memoir a boost: *timing*.

Again. Like me, you can probably count the ways that the
COVID pandemic *hasn't* adversely effected mental health
issues on less than one hand: depression, loneliness, domestic
violence, etc. All worse with the pandemic.

Up to 40% of Americans are experiencing mental health
problems. And get this: 11% have seriously considered killing
themselves. While I'm not particularly proud of it, most of
these pathologies (*except* domestic violence—you can ask my

wife) are old friends of mine. As are the psychiatric treatments and some of the medications used to combat them.

So, you could say I'm in a position of being able to speak from long experience as a survivor. But, more important, I can speak as someone who's managed not just to survive, but even thrive. Married for decades. A productive career, including eight years in the Colorado legislature. A wonderful family, including six grandkids.

HAPPY TRAILS TO YOU!

Of course, I don't know how you'll respond to this post. My intent is that it will be an encouragement in difficult times. But there've been dark stretches in my life when I would have deeply resented its relentless chirpiness. To which I'll reply with a line I learned years ago in Amway that was supposed to be a foolproof way of overcoming objections: "I know how you feel. I felt the same way. But here's what I found."

And what did I find? Someday this pandemic will end. Just like *Little Orphan Annie* sings: "You can bet your bottom dollar that tomorrow there'll be sun!"

And perhaps even more of a solace? The American people are remarkably resilient: a Civil War, two World Wars, a grinding Great Depression, civil unrest. You name it. We've emerged from them all. And usually, stronger than before.

So, has COVID been tough? Absolutely. But will America somehow emerge stronger than ever?

I guess you know how I'm betting.

BIRDS OF A FEATHER

I first heard about her killing herself when I was at Mom's late one spring afternoon. The sun was slanting through her bedroom window, the motes slowly drifting down through the brilliant shaft of light.

"Did you hear," she began, "that Lolly committed suicide?"

"You're kidding," I said, looking at her.

"What happened? Didn't she have some kids?"

"Yes," she replied, "they had three. But her husband was unfaithful time after time. I guess she just couldn't take it anymore."

"Oh, my," I responded.

And those may have been about the last two words I ever said out loud about Lolly. Until now. But her ghost has made regular visitations, haunting the recesses of memory, even while she was very much alive.

THE UGLY DUCKLING

I'd known her since elementary school. At that age, Lolly was all gangly legs beneath rubbery, articulate lips and raven black hair. To say that her form at that young age was marred wouldn't be an exaggeration—at least to me. I never gave her a second, schoolboy look. Or, for that matter, thought. What she thought of me at that point, I'm not entirely sure. But I doubt my feelings were reciprocated.

In appearance, I was her opposite. Blond locks that bleached to white around the sun drenched Crestmoor neighborhood swimming pool where I spent so many Denver summer days as a kid. My conventional, even pretty, good looks were my endowment from a set of handsome parents.

It might just be my imagination speaking—or pride—but I seem to recall twitterings among the little girls at school about what a cute boy he is. And Lolly was one of those girls. But what she, or the other girls who knew me, thought about my appearance didn't really much matter. If it was a female, especially a cute one, I was pretty much in mortal terror as I grew into those pitifully awkward teenage years. And when we went our separate ways in junior high, she was out of sight. And even further out of mind.

THE TERMINAL BAR

The summer before I transferred to Colorado University at Boulder, I worked digging ditches for Slim Manley in what was then known as the town of Hideaway Park, just over the Continental Divide from Denver, a few miles west of the Winter Park ski area. I rented a bedroom in a weary mobile home squatting off US 40 in a grove of spindly lodge pole pines next door to the long-gone diner Edna's Kitchen.

A hundred feet beyond my bedroom window, the tracks of the Denver & Rio Grande Rail Road labored up the Frazier River valley to the base of the ski area where they bent east before plunging into the Stygian, reeking darkness of the Moffat Tunnel for the six-mile-long slog to the east side of the Continental Divide. And I'd know. As a boy, every Saturday during the season, I rode the train to Winter Park with the

Eskimo Ski Club along with hundreds of other kids. Little angels we weren't. More like the hellions right out of central casting from *Pinocchio's* Pleasure Island.

Hijinks were the order of the day as the train glided away from the Winter Park siding after a day of skiing bound for Denver and home. The stench of damp wool, orange peels, and tuna fish sandwiches ground to a pulp under snowy ski boots, along with faintly illuminated tendrils of diesel fumes, were our fellow passengers until we emerged long minutes later into the late afternoon sunlight at the east portal of the tunnel. My big sister, Linda, was a "counselor" on the train in exchange for her lift ticket.

Driving us to lower downtown in the predawn darkness in the folks' 1950 gray Ford coupe, my sister parked around the corner from Union Station near the Terminal Bar. When the name of the saloon, in my naive mind, didn't signify the end of the line as much as the raggedy men who haunted nearby, shadowy doorways, clinging to the ends of their ropes. That was a time when the area still would have been recognized by the outcast "beat" characters that drifted through Denver in the pages of Jack Kerouac's classic, *On The Road*. Rather than the now-gleaming art deco yuppie watering hole that, like so much else in the "new" Denver, has pilfered the name, but not the spirit, of the cow town I knew growing up.

SLIM

"Well," Slim Manley announced as he climbed out of his blue-faded-to-gray Ford pickup on a bright June 20 morning as I steeled myself for another day digging ditches, "winter's on its way." Which meant something at nine thousand feet just outside Hideaway Park and within earshot of the trains that still labored up the Frasier River valley, past the now grassy, wild-flower-strewn ski trails of Winter Park. And where the rails still bent into the Moffat Tunnel.

But it was ten years on. A seeming eternity to a college kid, whose fond winter memories had drawn him back to a town that lured fun seekers year-round. Hikers. Backpackers. Dime store cowboys and girls at dude ranches. And me? A distinctly unglamorous summer job digging ditches for sewer and water lines to service vacation homes that were springing up around the ski resort like mushrooms after a summer cloud burst.

From where I went to work outside of Hideaway Park, you could look up at the Continental Divide just to the east and see snow fields that would linger until winter closed in again. Aside from his memorable aphorisms, there wasn't much to like about working down in Slim's ditches. It wasn't so much that the work was physically demanding; it bored me to somnambulism.

While Slim, Wizard of Oz like, manipulated the levers of the yellow, WWII vintage backhoe behind me, I sat in the driver's cab up front, pulling forward a few feet at the sound of one "Beep!" And reversing a few feet at the sound of "Beep! Beep!" Until, that is, the gentle lurching and the subdued roar of the contraption lulled me to sleep beneath the warm afternoon sun.

It didn't happen often, but I still remember Slim storming up to my seat and yelling "Wake up!" at my head that was slumped on my chest when I'd failed to respond to his insistent "Beep! Beep!" Why didn't he fire me?

In retrospect, it seems pretty obvious: he couldn't find anyone else who'd reliably turn up and climb into the driver's seat of that ancient backhoe through the brief, summer construction season. Even if, occasionally, I was asleep at the wheel.

THE BLACK SWAN

Thirty miles north of where Slim's backhoe worried away at the boulder-speckled soil that was both his bread and butter and the bane of his existence, near the headwaters of the Colorado River, there's a dude ranch that's been around nearly a hundred years: the C Lazy U.

I never made it up there, but it's got to operate on pretty much the same, seasonal lines that characterize the other mountain attractions that rely heavily on tourism: high school and college kids to do the grunt work of waiting tables, cleaning guest rooms, washing dishes, mucking stables for trail horses. Digging ditches. And that's how I crossed paths with Lolly again.

Somehow, as summer drew to a close, we both got word of a party at a vacation home in Hideaway Park. "Lolly?" I asked over the din of a long-forgotten cut from . . . what? The Rolling Stones were big then.

"I haven't seen you since our Graland days in sixth grade. What are you doing up here?"

"Well," she said, wrapping her lips around the word and leaning in to make herself heard, "I'm working at the C Lazy U on the other side of Grandby."

Through the stench of cigarette smoke and sour beer, I caught a whiff of her perfume; I learned later that it was White Shoulders. And that her shampoo was the flower child version of Herbal Essence. I won't mention the acrid taste of her mouth.

"Some of us heard about the party and came down. What are you doing here?"

"I've got a summer job digging ditches in this neighborhood. Hideaway Park is putting in new water and sewer lines. Really glamorous work. Slim Manley's the old guy I work for; he lives in Grandby. I'll be heading back down to Boulder in a couple of weeks. I'm taking a year off school to try to do some writing. I'm renting a house with some guys I know from school."

"Yeah," she replied, "I'm going back to CU in a few weeks

myself. Some friends and I have a rented house up on The Hill."

"Well," I said, "maybe we can get together sometime. Do you have a phone there yet?"

"We do. Let me write it out for you."

"Great. Maybe I'll give you a call."

Not much came of that brief encounter. Unless you fail to count that the ugly duckling had morphed into the black swan.

TIME'S A WASTIN'

"Hello, can I speak with Lolly?"

"Yes, she's right here. Let me give her the phone."

"Hello?"

"Lolly, this is Spencer Swalm," I began. "We ran into each other last summer in Hideaway Park. You gave me your number. I'm calling to see if you'd like to go dancing sometime."

And just like that, before the weekend was over, we'd ridden to a swing dance club north of Boulder in my used VW Bug. The name of the club? No idea; it's long gone. But we enjoyed ourselves, awkward though we were, holding hands, rocking back and forth, spinning in and out of a clench, ducking under each other's arms.

I was far from accomplished in leading such intricate maneuvers. But, by comparison to the others around us on the crowded dance floor who gyrated in place and never seemed to touch, I imagined we were hot stuff. When the band took a break, we stepped out of the steamy club's back door and into the sweat-chilled night air on the flagstone paved patio.

To the west, not far beyond the faint shadows cast by the string of naked light bulbs dangling overhead, the Front Range heaved up. Beyond it, the ragged summits of the Indian Peaks marched north along the Continental Divide, soaring over thirteen thousand feet into the star spangled darkness: Apache, Arikaree, Kiowa, Navajo, Ogalalla, Pawnee. Before I drove her home, we'd grown comfortable in each other's arms.

But away from the dance floor, our relationship was shrouded in a cloud of unknowing. A relationship built on sand, one of groping in the dark. But that was the least of my worries. My conscience stalked me at every turn; it tormented me. And I had no idea why. Or that there even was such a thing as a conscience.

Having drunk deeply from the dregs of what was left of the liberated '60s, by 1973 I was thoroughly coarsened. When a guy who lived next door crudely asserted of women that "a unit is a unit," I may have been inwardly repelled. But far be it from me to do anything other than snicker and play along. Anything rather than betraying myself as a backward moralizer.

Like Macbeth, I must have hoped that those nagging qualms would vanish with "hard use." But even though I was "young in deed," they didn't. They only got worse. Again and again, we broke up. And made up. Like ripping off a scab. Over and over.

Incredibly, the thought of marriage never even crossed my benighted mind. What did *that* have to do with my gratification? Or, to put it more plainly, my *selfish* gratification? Nothing. Not even worth a passing thought. But in the end, our relationship didn't break. I did. Or, at least, I *started* to break.

When the next summer came, Lolly went abroad to study in Europe.

THE GOOD DOCTOR

It wasn't long before Lolly got back from her European trip that the bluegrass legend Doc Watson and his son, Merle, did a show at Boulder's now long-gone Tulagi's night club. I drove into town and found a stool at the back of the dimly lit bar. I danced with a nearby woman. Took her home for the night. And never saw her again. Although I got a wistful card from her a week later: "Thinking of you."

In her book, *Bird By Bird: Some Instructions On Writing And Life*, Anne Lamont_says this about writing about stuff you (meaning, of course, *me*) don't want to write about:

> Life is lukewarm enough! Give us a little heat! If I'm going to read about a bunch of people who drive Volkswagens and seem to have mostly Volkswagen-sized problems, and the writer shows there's a lot of very, very cold water down below, I eventually want for someone to crash through. I want people who write confusing and hard to see. I want writers to plunge through those holes and in spaces around them exist all sorts of possibility, including the chance to see who we are and to glimpse the mystery."

You want to see crashed through? Feel the icy depths beneath? Try this.

Before Lolly got home, I went to the medical clinic on the CU campus and got myself tested for VD. I got a clean bill of health. But so what? If there's a way to feel cheaper and dirtier, I don't want to hear about it. But when Lolly got back to Boulder, I found out that there *is* a way to feel cheaper and dirtier.

I told Lolly about it one day when we were driving through Boulder in that old VW.

"I had sex with a woman while you were gone. I always assumed you and Charlie were having sex. Isn't that so?"

"It absolutely isn't," she shot back, glaring over at me. "He was only a friend. I've known him for years."

I've no reason to believe she didn't get herself tested also.

THE GIFT HORSE

That was the last I ever saw of Lolly. Until, that is, the time I drove to the new place she was renting with some other women near the start of the next school year. I parked my VW in front of the house, pulled the guitar case out of the back seat, climbed the steps to the front porch and knocked.

"Hi," I said to the woman who answered the door, "I'm Spencer Swalm. Can I speak with Lolly?"

"Lolly?" she called, looking over her shoulder, "someone's here to see you."

As she approached through the house, it was if she were walking through a dimly lit tunnel before she emerged into the brilliant sun of the front porch.

"Hello," she said, her lips wrapping around the word before they snapped shut. I waited. But she said nothing, looking beyond me to the street behind. "I hope you're well."

I paused again, glancing over my shoulder to see what had caught her attention. A car went by. I looked down at the guitar case.

"I've been working with a guy at a guitar repair shop down the street here. I fixed up a guitar and brought it by for you. It's not perfect. But I brought it by for you," I said, lifting the case toward her.

"Thanks," she replied, not taking the case handle. "Why don't you leave it out here?" She gestured to a stack of old newspapers on the porch that were held down by a brick.

"Okay." Boulder's notorious for its ferocious wind. I put the guitar case on the other side of the stack of newspapers. "Maybe I'll see you around sometime," I said before walking back down the stairs.

Before I got to the bottom, the door closed behind me. I never saw her again. And neither will anyone else this side of eternity.

THE REASON WHY?

Yes, Lolly and I were physically attracted to one another. But was there more to it than that? If you work backward, perhaps it's likely.

I labored under a miasma of unknowing. But, in our early twenties, we were scarcely more than kids. Why would she have been any more self-aware? I was bipolar but completely clueless.

On the heels of a hunting trip with my dad that went badly off the rails, he was able to convince a judge to have me involuntarily committed to a psychiatric hospital for three weeks. When I got out, I almost immediately quit taking the medication prescribed to control the disorder. And, within a few years —and with three young kids of my own—I was routinely flirting with the idea of suicide myself.

It was years before I came to grips with my own illness, began routinely seeing a psychiatrist, and taking the prescribed drugs. Every night.

Did Lolly and I, instinctively, recognize one another as kindred spirits? Was that the real basis of the attraction? I can't know. But why would a woman with three little children, the daughter of a physician herself, despite a husband that was serially unfaithful, kill herself? Why not just get a divorce? Again, I can't know.

But I do know that in the throes of a bipolar depression, what looks completely insane to a normal person on the outside looking in, might seem like the only way out to a person trapped on the inside and desperate for a way to get out. In the depths of despair, with three young children, she killed herself.

ABOUT THE AUTHOR

Born and bred in Colorado, Spencer Swalm has seen his state go from a rural backwater to—for better or worse—a vibrant national trendsetter. As a member of the state's House of Representatives, Swalm was more than a passive observer of the changes that shaped Colorado during the course of his life. He helped set the course of some of those changes.

Emerging from a personal crisis, Swalm underwent a dramatic conversion to Christianity as a young man. But his newly found faith wasn't a panacea; the irrational highs and life-threatening lows of bipolar disorder continued to periodically dog his steps. Reading, at times, like either a comedy or a tragedy, Swalm went from being involuntarily committed to a psychiatric hospital, to a madcap fling with Amway that sent him and his wife careening from coast to coast in search of elusive riches in the soap business.

Stymied at every turn, Swalm turned his back on a failing law practice before finding modest success in the insurance business. The ultimate solution to the financial woes? An inheritance from his rags-to-riches father that gave him the financial freedom to pursue his passion for politics and writing. As the fruit of four hard-fought, closely contested elections, Swalm served eight years in the Colorado House of Representatives. Drawing on those diverse experiences, Swalm began blogging athttps://outsidelookingin4u.comin anticipation of writing his memoir.